Public-Private Collaborations for Long-Term Investments

T0327590

This book is dedicated to:

My parents, who taught me to take nothing for granted,
and who nurtured the ethics, the care, and passion I have
for everything I do.
Velia, my mentor, in life and at work.
Francesca and Niccolò, colleagues but above all my family.
Veronica

My mum, an example of strength and tenderness at the same time.
My dad, for his continuous guidance from the other side of life.
My beloved Angelo, for his persistence and long-term vision.
Francesca

Those who care for the future.
Niccolò

Public-Private Collaborations for Long-Term Investments
Converging Towards Public Value Generation

Veronica Vecchi

Full Professor of Practice of Government, Health and Not for Profit, SDA Bocconi School of Management, Italy

Francesca Casalini

Junior Lecturer of Government, Health and Not for Profit, SDA Bocconi School of Management, Italy, and Research Assistant of Systemic Management and Public Governance, University of St. Gallen, Switzerland

Niccolò Cusumano

Associate Professor of Practice of Government, Health and Not for Profit, SDA Bocconi School of Management, Italy

Edward Elgar
PUBLISHING

Cheltenham, UK • Northampton, MA, USA

Published by
Edward Elgar Publishing Limited
The Lypiatts
15 Lansdown Road
Cheltenham
Glos GL50 2JA
UK

Edward Elgar Publishing, Inc.
William Pratt House
9 Dewey Court
Northampton
Massachusetts 01060
USA

Paperback edition 2023

A catalogue record for this book
is available from the British Library

Library of Congress Control Number: 2022937617

This book is available electronically in the **Elgar**online
Political Science and Public Policy subject collection
http://dx.doi.org/10.4337/9781802205619

ISBN 978 1 80220 560 2 (cased)
ISBN 978 1 80220 561 9 (eBook)
ISBN 978 1 0353 2212 1 (paperback)

Printed and bound by CPI Group (UK) Ltd, Croydon, CR0 4YY

Contents

Tables

Boxes

Foreword
Iliyana Tsanova, Deputy Director-General – DG Budget, European Commission

I have been a guest lecturer at the course on Long-Term Investments and PPP at Bocconi University for a few years now. When I was first invited, I was asked to introduce students to the European Fund for Strategic Investments (EFSI) and share my experience as its Deputy Managing Director. At that time, EFSI was an innovative instrument and the first real pan-European response to the massive economic and social challenge that the European Union (EU) was facing as a consequence of the global financial and economic crisis of 2008. This instrument revolutionized how public funding can be used to mobilize capital and catalyze long-term investments with high value added for the people and the economy. We have enabled investments of more than 500 billion euros in the period of 2015 to 2020 by providing debt and equity financings for research and development, sustainable infrastructure, and support to start-ups, small and medium firms, and large corporates. EFSI clearly demonstrated that any economic recovery package can be fully in line with sustainability and environmental, social and governance (ESG) objectives. Presently, the European Green Deal is the new growth strategy for Europe and is at the heart of the Covid-19 post-pandemic recovery support under the Next Generation EU program.

This book touches precisely on these points – the importance of an effective collaboration between private and public stakeholders to create public value and foster long-term investments to support the green and sustainable transition. The investments required to achieve climate neutrality and sustainable development targets are estimated to be trillions of euros. However, the challenges are not only financial as, for example, we cannot achieve these goals with the existing technologies. Therefore, we must invest in innovative and ground-breaking technologies that should be affordable and accessible to everyone; we have to ensure that the green transition is inclusive, and that no one is left behind. As this book argues, the achievement of these common objectives requires networking and collaboration between public and private stakeholders on many levels, for which it presents various partnership mechanisms and frameworks.

An important EU policy initiative, the EU Sustainable Finance Strategy and Taxonomy, is expected to trigger a substantial change in the investment mindset of the private sector. Going forward, business strategies, investment decisions, and policy choices need to factor in the ESG objectives. The policy push will channel private and public capital to environmentally sustainable investments and unlock the full potential of capital markets to achieve the climate and sustainability goals. This trend is clearly recognized in the book, where various angles and approaches for the ESG and impact investing are explored in Chapter 2.

The book also focuses on the necessity to use blended finance solutions to catalyze investments and mobilize private capital in areas and markets affected by failures or to achieve the right risk/return profile to enable investments. I can confidently say that the public support from the EU and national budgets has been pivotal in sustaining risk capital across the EU, when it suffered from investment gaps in the last decade. Investments were enabled through various financial instruments such as the blending of financial resources, fund of funds to support innovative companies, risk-sharing instruments, and guarantees to commercial and national development banks, taking subordinated positions for project finance transactions and venture debt investments for growth companies, to name a few. The book provides a comprehensive overview of the plethora of existing blending mechanisms.

I believe that this book, written with great passion and a competence grounded in academic research and a deep hands-on experience by Veronica, Francesca and Niccolò, will be an excellent reference to university and master students, executives and civil servants, academic researchers, and many others who are keen to learn more about enabling long-term investments and public-private collaborations.

To sustain long-term investments and the generation of public value, as well as to accelerate the achievement of the Sustainable Development Goals, we all need to share a common background and vision. This book can be the right starting point for this challenging and urgent co-evolution.

Preface

The idea to write this book came in 2018 during the course "Long-Term Investments and Public-Private Partnerships," taught at Bocconi University by Veronica and her friend and colleague Giovanni Gorno Tempini, and it became a reality in the wake of the Covid-19 pandemic, which highlighted the importance of sustainable development and long-term investing.

The necessity to adopt a long-term investment approach is certainly not new, even if it started to gain growing interest in the policy and business arena after the great financial crisis of 2007–2008. Over the past decade, one of the main criticisms circulating in the public market is that this forces companies to obsessively look at quarterly results, rather than promote durable business models and long-term innovation. Instead, the global environmental crisis and economic inequalities require transformative action. There is growing recognition that financial performance cannot be decoupled from broader environmental and societal issues. Elevating corporate social responsibility from a responsive to a strategic level, and developing new investment approaches like Environmental, Society and Governance (ESG) and impact investing are unavoidable trends.

The UN 2030 Agenda for Sustainable Development, which defines the global Sustainable Development Goals (SDGs), in order to empower people, protect the planet, promote prosperity and peace, recognizes the importance of partnerships.

Governments and market players therefore seem to be converging, through different patterns of collaboration, towards a generation of more value for the society at large. In the book we refer to this concept with the expression "public value", which can be operationalized through the SDGs, as critical areas where public and private investments should converge in the upcoming years to tackle urgent societal issues.

If collaborations are crucial to generate the needed public value, a recurrent term in the global policy agenda and across business roundtables, it is salient to understand how these collaborations can take place. The book, in Chapter 1, offers two linked frameworks where collaborations are organized into three levels: policy (macro), program (meso), and project (micro). Each level is characterized by different cooperation mechanisms that can be used to spur long-term investment. The book guides readers through some areas of public-private collaboration, not only with the aim of explaining their rationale and features but mainly to stimulate governments and market players to co-evolve, and therefore make significant advancement in the way in which they collaborate and partner up together. We firmly believe that regulation, incentives, and different forms of collaboration, based on mutual public-private push/pull actions, could expand and channel the blooming societal interest shown by financial investors and corporations.

A remarkably interesting debate is becoming apparent about the true nature of such refocus. Is it a marketing gimmick that could just generate green societal washing or is there a clear view that trying to solve societal issues can act as a massive new driver for competitive advantage, as Michael Porter spread through the label of 'shared value creation'? Will ESG investments move from a nice to have add-on into a real sustainable approach aiming to generate some sort of financial+social+environmental additionality? What will impact investing be, and what will the differences between ESG/sustainable finance and impact investing be? Will they be able, in different ways and through different ranges of public-private collaboration, to achieve the SDGs?

We all, policymakers, investors, public and private managers, citizens, and scholars, can be the live-action characters of the capacity of different institutions to shape a better future for the next generations and to provide the right answers to such questions.

This book offers a panorama of such trends in Chapter 2 (dedicated to sustainability in public and private organizations and ESG investing) and in Chapter 3 (dedicated to impact investing, from an investor and investee perspective), with the aim to shed light on the importance of a long-term perspective in public- and private-sector decision making.

Investing with a long-term perspective and, above all, for the achievement of the SDGs is certainly risky and requires a massive amount of money, which cannot be provided by public organizations alone. Blended finance mechanisms, as a form of meso-level partnership, can play a salient role in this landscape. Across the world, in emerging and mature economies, blended finance mechanisms have been put in place, with different structures and goals (and sometimes with different names). Chapter 4 is dedicated to this immensely powerful form of financial partnership.

Long-term investments are not only about infrastructure, even though it is one of the main forms, where collaboration has been playing a crucial role for decades, through public-private partnerships in a strict sense, mainly applied to economic infrastructure. Governments across the world, after failures of such forms of collaboration, are trying to find other ways to attract private investment in infrastructure, and the big challenge regards mainly social and intangible infrastructure. We do not like the "changing the name" or "rebranding" approach and we feel that this could be the risk. There are only three ways to deliver and operate infrastructure: the in-house traditional approach, the hybrid approach (based on institutional and contractual partnerships), and privatization in context where competition in the market is possible. To provide an answer to those policymakers who are looking for alternatives, we have written Chapter 5, which, in the first part, adopts a sort of "back to square one" approach, where we show that the only way to attract private capital when privatization is not an option is through a contractual partnership. Of course, it has to be structured with different approaches than those used in the past; in a nutshell, with a "horses for courses" mindset, because context and sector features do matter. Although it requires immense intellectual and professional effort to structure a good public-private partnership contract, we believe that it is possible, and Chapter 6 offers some hints on the main crucial issues to structure a sustainable contract. The chapter gathers the main elements discussed in our previous book *Public Private Partnerships for Sustainable Contracts.*

All these topics have been discussed in the last years in many executive courses and masters that we teach at the Bocconi University School of Management, where we all work; some of them (especially contractual public-private partnerships and impact investing) have also been the focus of our own academic research and scientific papers.

Finally, the book includes some quotes on the relevance of the topic written by the main players, some of them friends with whom we have worked or who have been keynote speakers in our courses.

We do hope this book can enlighten and stimulate you to think and work differently, for the next generations.

Acknowledgments

Writing a book is a journey but when you have to finalize it, you steal time from your family and friends. Therefore, my warmest thanks is for Barbara and Paola, who have been so kind to tolerate my last-second cancellations; Lori, who always makes me sparkle with stunning dresses; Ale, one of my best friends, who trains me without a tomorrow to build *corpore sano et mens sana*; Andrea, for the amazing bike tours that are a mix of sweat and history; and my beloved colleague and friend, la Sapo, who always brightens my mind and heals my soul. A special thought goes also to Angelo, a gift that appeared along a journey "without a specific destination."

Veronica

This book would not have been possible without the imagination and efforts of Veronica. She is the smartest and most enthusiast colleague I could ever ask for, as well as a friend and mentor. Therefore, I really want to thank her for envisioning this book and turning it into reality, and for always pushing me out of my comfort zone. I also want to thank my colleague Kuno Schedler for his continuous guidance and support for my professional development.

Francesca

We all thank the experts that provided constructive comments for the development of this book, as well as the quotes on the relevance of the topic. In alphabetical order, we would like to offer thanks to Guido Bichisao, Royston Braganza, Nelson Chang, Raffaele Della Croce, Damien Dunn, Giovanni Gorno Tempini, Marie Lam-Frendo, Dario Scannapieco, Davide Serra, Iliyana Tsanova, and Maria Teresa Zappia. We also thank Rachel for her support in proofreading and the encouragement she gave to Veronica to start a new book, and Lorenzo, for valuable support with the submission.

Veronica, Francesca, and Niccolò

Abbreviations

AfDB	African Development Bank
ASEAN	Association of Southeast Asian Nations
AuM	assets under management
BF	blended finance
CA	contracting authority
CEO	chief executive officer
CGIF	credit guarantee and investment facility
CGS	credit guarantee schemes
CPPP	contractual public-private partnership
CSR	corporate social responsibility
CSV	creating shared value
DBFMO	design, build, finance, maintain, and operate
DIB	development impact bond
DSCR	debt service coverage ratio
EA	economic additionality
EIB	European Investment Bank
EIF	European Investment Fund
EO	economic operator
EU	European Union
FA	financial additionality
FCG	Fondo Centrale di Garanzia
FONADIN	Fondo Nacional de Infraestructura
GIIN	Global Impact Investing Network
HNWI	high-net-worth individual
HRADF	Hellenic Republic Asset Development Fund
II	impact investing
IMM	impact measurement and management

JAWEF	Japan ASEAN Women Empowerment Fund
LTInv	long-term investors
LTIs	long-term investments
MDBs	multilateral development banks
MES	medical equipment service
MFI	micro-finance institution
MGI	mutual guarantee institution
OECD	Organisation for Economic Co-operation and Development
PPP	public-private partnerships
R&D	research and development
SBA	Small Business Administration
SBIC	Small Business Investment Company
SDGs	Sustainable Development Goals
SIA	social impact accelerator
SIB	social impact bond
SMEs	small and medium-sized enterprises
SoE	state-owned enterprise
SPV	special purpose vehicle
SRI	socially responsible investing
UK	United Kingdom
US	United States
VC	venture capital
VfM	value for money
VfP	value for people

Expert quotes

"The business of business is being redefined before our very eyes: inclusion, sustainability, impact, and ESG are now integrated into most investment decisions. Much more needs to be done as Agenda 2030 will not be met till 'all hands are on deck'. Public Private Collaboration is one crucial element of this approach. Our pioneering SDG Impact Bonds have demonstrated that multiple stakeholders – corporates, social enterprises, government, capital market players, philanthropists, etc. – can come together to make long-lasting and real impact."

Royston Braganza, Chief Executive Officer, Grameen Capital

"Infrastructure will be a core engine of post-pandemic recovery. Long-term financial institutions are ready to take a stake in this challenge and foster quality infrastructure investment for the future of Europe. Thanks to the resources mobilized through the NGEU and the consequent catalytic effect for private resources, in the next months and years the blending between public and private resources will be highly encouraged.

Our mission is crucial, as a bridge between the private and public sectors, to finance the increasing global infrastructure investment gap and unleash the great potential of private investments in green and quality infrastructure. We must work as an accelerator of infrastructure investment projects through loans to public bodies and companies, advisory services and promotion of Public Private Collaboration investments, and by encouraging the private sector to pursue new investments in the sector."

Dario Scannapieco, Chief Executive Officer and General Manager,
Cassa Depositi e Prestiti

"De-risking mechanisms, the blending of public and private resources such as the use of financial guarantees and junior loans, are crucial to allow for the multiplication of financial resources and reduce the perceived risk for private investors. This allows a greater involvement of private investors in long-term investments and a better risk allocation. Today, one of the major hurdles to large-scale cooperation between public and private sectors is represented by the complexity of Public Private Collaboration contracts, which have proven challenging to prepare, procure, and deliver. Development financial institu-

tions, pursuing their essential role as a bridge between the private and public sector, could be at the forefront to boost quality investments ... and mitigate the risk for the private sector."
Giovanni Gorno Tempini, Chairman, Cassa Depositi e Prestiti and Adjunct Professor of Long Term Investment and PPP at Bocconi University

"Infrastructure is the backbone of economies worldwide. Yet, even as many countries turn to infrastructure stimulus to help drive the COVID-19 recovery, the USD15 trillion global infrastructure financing gap stands as a stark reminder of what the public sector has not been able to achieve alone. Activating private capital is key to closing this gap and the industry needs to explore investment options and create stronger partnerships between the public and private sectors. This will help to drive economic recovery in the short term whilst driving longer-term economic and social outcomes."
Marie Lam-Frendo, Chief Executive Officer, Global Infrastructure Hub

"At a time when infrastructure investments are a key instrument for economic recovery and governments have approved large programs, this book provides an excellent framework to understand how infrastructure investments work and the role of the main actors in this domain. The importance of a close collaboration by the main stakeholders on such long-term investments is greatly described to provide a very useful analysis of public value creation and how it is evolving to address the challenges of our time."
Guido Bichisao, Director Head of Counterparty Management, Transaction, and Restructuring Directorate, European Investment Bank

"In this era, we need to awaken a compassion of planetary scale and think globally. Facing the epidemic, climate change, and moving toward a more ideal society, our thinking needs to change from 'I' to 'Us'. The capitalized 'WE' is the necessary step for mankind to move towards a more sustainable future. The core problem that mankind faces is: how do we protect the Earth, clean it, and deliver it to future generations more perfectly?"
Nelson Chang, Chairman, Taiwan Cement Corporation

"Nowadays everyone talks about sustainability looking more at opportunities and less at costs. The danger of greenwashing is around the corner. The green transition that awaits us in the next 30 years will be expensive, but that does not detract from the possibility for patient investors to achieve a solid performance."
Davide Serra, Founder and Chief Executive Officer, Algebris Investments

"The impact investing market has moved from billions to trillions if we look at 2020 data. This refers to an expanded definition of impact investing which combs measured impact with intended impact. Within the impact investing market blended finance and the importance of mobilizing private capital has become even more relevant in a COVID-19 environment. Development banks, multilaterals, and bilateral governments have stepped in to provide de-risking measures in emerging and frontier markets and attract flows from institutional investors now even more needed to scale up activities and achieve the UN SDGs by 2030."

Maria Teresa Zappia, Deputy Chief Executive Officer,
BlueOrchard Finance

"Project proponents will often assign an element of sovereign risk to infrastructure projects, such as the unanticipated changes of government regulation. However, to consider this risk as exogenous to a project ignores the underlying motivation of government regulators – which is to respond to societies' values (be it clean air, open spaces, safety). The most effective way to anticipate and understand those values is a public-private collaboration where the project proponent actively seeks to incorporate the views of stake-holders. Understanding and meeting stakeholder demands should not be seen as short-term costs, but rather as long-term insurance. Regulatory risk will undoubtedly be lower in the long run. Companies will also pursue Corporate Social Responsibility, which is not simple altruism, but another approach to de-risking long-term projects by aligning to society's values."

Damien Dunn, Principal Adviser, Infrastructure at the Australian Treasury
and Past Chair of the OECD Long Term Investment Working Group

"Long-term investment can foster inclusive growth and a green recovery. This book is topical in explaining how to leverage this opportunity analyzing new forms of collaboration among public and private actors."

Raffaele Della Croce, Senior Economist OECD – Long Term Investment

1. Public-private partnerships for long-term investments: the context and the framework

1. LONG-TERM INVESTMENTS FOR PUBLIC VALUE CREATION

Events such as the recession following the global financial crisis of 2007–2008, followed by the need to achieve the Sustainable Development Goals (SDGs) formalized in 2015, and more recently the societal and economic challenges generated by the Covid-19 pandemic have highlighted the fundamental role of long-term investments (LTIs) and public-private partnerships (PPP).

LTIs can be defined as investments with the expectation of holding an asset for an indefinite period of time by an investor with the capability to do so. Typically, an LTI is expected to be held for at least 10 years or through an entire business cycle (World Economic Forum, 2011).

Long-term assets, which include major infrastructure investments, direct investments into unlisted companies, early-stage start-ups (i.e., direct private equity and venture capital), and strategic stakes in public companies, have a number of characteristics that attract long-term investors (LTInv) and, conversely, deter short-term investors, including the need for large upfront costs and the difficulty to sell in the short term at a price the investor would regard as fair (World Economic Forum, 2011).

From a financial perspective, investments defined as LTIs require capital with key characteristics (Della Croce et al., 2011):

- patient – being able to retain assets for a long period of time;
- productive – aiming at investing in productive activities critical for a sustainable growth, such as cleaner energies, infrastructure, and venture capital;
- engaged – with a professional attitude and competence to manage all possible risks, among them also environmental risks during the investment life; and
- motivated – the desire to create a transformation.

The benefits of LTIs are:

- for investors, LTIs can deliver better returns due to access to structural risk premia (i.e., market risk premium, liquidity premium, complexity premium), by taking advantage of secular themes/macro trends (i.e., themes such as aging societies, which will give rise to business opportunities not in a particular year/period, but in the long run), and the impact on corporate decision making;
- for corporations, LTIs can increase resilience, growth, and risk mitigation, as their managers have less pressure to fulfil short-term goals and can focus more on long-term value creation (e.g., they tend to be more inclined to increase research and development (R&D) spending);
- for governments, LTIs are crucial to implement strategic and bold public policies to ensure the public interest, such as those underpinning the achievement of SDGs; and
- for society at large, LTIs can provide "social goods" such as the stabilization of financial markets, promotion of sustainable and equitable growth, and a generation of wider economic, social, and environmental benefits.

The focus of this book is on LTIs that promote economic, societal, and environmental development (what we call "public value"). In this sense, it deals not only with LTIs in economic infrastructure such as transport and mobility, energy, telecom and connectivity, and social infrastructure, including education, research, housing, and healthcare, but also with strategic corporate investments in R&D and direct investments in new business development.

Actors playing as LTInv are both financial and non-financial.

Financial LTInv include not only public institutions, and among them two of the most important LTInv such as promotional/multilateral development banks (as financial arms of governments or public institutions) and sovereign wealth funds, but more and more also private asset owners with suitable longer-term liability profiles, such as family offices, endowments, foundations, pension funds, and life insurers. The assets of such LTInv are managed by mutual funds, private equity firms, and other asset management firms. ESG (environmental, social, and governance) and impact investing, underpinned by a long-term perspective, are becoming a dominant target for LTInv.

Among non-financial LTInv one of the most important is the public sector, which invests in the long term to generate positive economic, environmental, and social return; this is intrinsic to its mission. For corporates, the concept of long-term value creation means that a company aims to optimize its financial, social, and environmental value in the long term, making it prepared for the transition to a more sustainable economic model (Tirole, 2017; Schoenmaker & Schramade, 2019). For decades, profit maximization has played a leading role in, corporate finance and business strategies. However, recent approaches (Hart & Zingales, 2017) suggest that shareholder welfare maximization should replace market value maximization. Environmental and social externalities can be internalized in the business strategy under the pressure of government regulation and taxation, society, and technological developments, such as low-cost solar and wind energy (Schoenmaker & Schramade, 2019). New evidence shows that ESG integration into investment can generate superior financial performance (e.g., Khan et al., 2016).

2.   THE IMPORTANCE OF PUBLIC-PRIVATE PARTNERSHIPS/COLLABORATIONS AS A DRIVER FOR LONG-TERM INVESTMENTS FOR PUBLIC VALUE CREATION

The SDGs, which are the pillars of the 2030 Agenda for Sustainable Development adopted by all United Nations member states in 2015, well describe the wicked problems of our contemporary society and the challenge for all stakeholders, both public and private. They require a coordinated effort of public and private players, through global partnerships, due to their complexity and magnitude.

In September 2019, United Nations Deputy Secretary-General Amina Mohammed said:

> Business leaders have a critical role to play ... I urge all companies to drive ambitious SDG actions throughout their operations and supply chains, embedding human rights, labor, environment, and anti-corruption into core business. Business and finance can lead through their actions and investment decisions on economic transformation that leaves no one behind. Meanwhile, governments must create the space for businesses to join them in transforming their economies and societies. Policymakers and regulators need to create a long-term investment environment for sustainable development that ensures fair and open trade, promotes the health and well-being of people and the planet, and protects human rights. Shareholders and citizens are already stepping up their demand for greener and more sustainable investments of their assets, and for greater sustainability disclosure to increase accountability and transparency. We want them to continue and to do more.

And later, in 2020:

> we have also seen unprecedented alliances, innovation, and achievements: rapid migration to digital technologies, a new generation of finance products and infrastructure, and ambitious social protection programs implemented at a scale never seen before. None of this would have been possible without partnerships. Indeed, Covid-19 has prompted extraordinary examples of collaboration on sustainable development.

Since their formalization, the SDGs represent the core of public policy agenda at both supranational and national levels across the world; also, investors are progressively shifting their focus towards a mid-/long-term perspective, with ESG investment approaches becoming dominant and sustainability issues becoming an integral part of corporate strategy. In this, the SDGs could be considered an institutionalized declination of public value, which is no longer limited to the public sector or the lone manager, as initially conceived by Moore (1995), but whose pursuit, given its magnitude and complexity, requires a coordinated mobilization of public and private stakeholders (Jørgensen & Bozeman, 2007; Meynhardt, 2009).

Public value creation indeed requires networking and collaboration. Crosby et al. (2017, p. 659) argue that public value can be pursued "not through the heroic efforts of strategic public managers, but through dispersed efforts and distributed leadership in which much of the enabling work can be performed by agents without formal authority in the government system." The failure of traditional forms of governmental intervention to manage the diversity of societal needs has called for more adaptable and networked forms of governance, which can be defined as "the commitment of a group of important actors from different sectors to a common agenda for solving a specific social problem" (Kania & Kramer, 2011, p. 36). In these networks of public and private actors, collaboration is based on the "linking or sharing of information, resources, activities, and capabilities of organizations to jointly achieve an outcome that the single organizations could not achieve separately" (Bryson et al., 2006).

More recently, this concept of collaboration and co-produced (public) value has been emphasized by Mazzucato (2021). She argues that it is necessary to reject the concept of "market failure" as a justification of government intervention in the market, and that "public value creation must involve the public sector setting a direction and public purpose for private and public actors to collaborate and innovate to solve societal problems." She defined this as a "market-shaping" and "market-creating" role of the public sector.

Also in this book, we argue that public value is not created in a vacuum, or through the efforts of a few actors. Partnerships are vital to attract private investors into LTIs with their enormous private wealth, which has reached its peak in recent years (in 2020, the stock of liquidity of high-net-worth individuals reached USD 79.5 trillion, almost equal to the world gross domestic product, with a compound annual growth rate in the period 2013–2020 of 5.8 percent[1]). They are also vital to attract risk-adverse LTInv in riskier projects, such as pension funds, whose assets have increased dramatically in the aftermath of the Covid-19 pandemic. Indeed, assets in retirement savings plans continued to grow in 2020 despite the shock of Covid-19, exceeding USD 56 trillion worldwide at year end and amounting to an 11 percent increase over 2019 figures. This growth was supported by an increase in the number of people participating in a retirement savings plan, an increase in the overall contributions into these plans, and positive investment returns in many countries (OECD, 2021b).

In this context, it urges the provision of a framework to understand how public-private collaboration supports LTI for the generation of public value.

3. THE PUBLIC-PRIVATE PARTNERSHIP FRAMEWORK

Over the last 20 years, public authorities and institutions have been experimenting with several mechanisms of PPP or collaborations to leverage the capital and the (potential) innovation capacity of the private sector. PPP has often been associated with a model to develop infrastructure (Hodge & Greve, 2017). However, we need to embrace a wider framework to understand how the public and private actors can partner together to realize that LTI is crucial for the achievement of the SDGs. Such partnerships can happen at policy, program, and project levels, as summarized in Figure 1.1.

Partnerships may be developed on three levels: macro, meso, and micro. Starting from the macro level, collaboration is informal and mainly aimed at framing and implementing a policy. In reality, the introduction and deployment of policies always happens through an articulated networking/collabora-

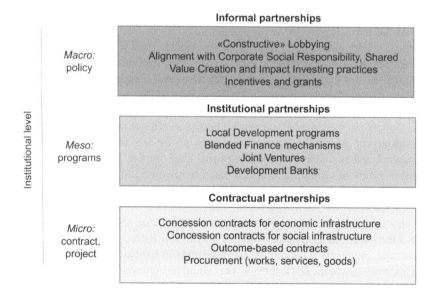

Figure 1.1   The public-private partnerships framework

tion between government or institutions and businesses, with the participation of third-party organizations, such as think tanks. At this level, an informal partnership can take the form of lobbying activities (transactional or relational) put in place by corporations, associations, or networks to influence the policymaking. Lobbying is not only aimed at postponing or preventing the introduction of a certain policy (law or regulation) that may increase corporate costs and therefore reduce profitability (at least in the short term), but also to stimulate the policymaker to introduce policies that can improve the competitive advantage of those corporations that are more innovative or that have more sophisticated business models. An example is a corporation that produces innovative systems for e-mobility fast charging that may decide to push and collaborate with governments to introduce, by law, the obligation to install such systems on high-speed roads and motorways, in order to accelerate the transition. A "constructive" lobbying for sustaining LTIs is generally done by those corporations and players that have conceived advanced practices in corporate social responsibility (CSR)/shared value creation, or by impact investors. In Chapter 2 we provide some examples of business leaders and investors that are looking for a better alignment between policymakers in order to accelerate the achievement of economic and societal policy goals (e.g., the SDGs). Social and societal challenges (such as global warming and environmental protection) are a terrain where public and private actors can work together (collaborate) to generate what is called public value. When public policies are designed to incentivize such efforts, also through grants and tax incentives to accelerate the transition, an innovative form of macro PPP can ensue.

At the meso level, PPP, with different degrees of intensity, create opportunities where public and private actors combine financial and non-financial resources to achieve a common goal. At this level we find, on one hand, institutional partnerships, such as public-private-owned companies/joint ventures (where the partnership is institutionalized through the setting up of a legal entity), and on the other hand, programs that have been co-designed and are co-implemented by public and private bodies to achieve social and economic development goals. These programs can be co-funded, or they can mobilize financial and non-financial assets towards such mutual goals. The level of formalization of such programs may vary significantly; for example, they can be implemented through associations or memorandums of understanding.

The rationale of partnering for the implementation of programs is not necessary to overcome financial constraints or to increase efficiency, which has been the dominant motivation with PPP in the New Public Management era. In this case, the primary goal of the partnership is to increase effectiveness, i.e., to improve outcomes and outreach. This could be achieved not only due to the superior competence and innovation capacity of the private sector but, above all, from the fact that the partnership allows institutions and stakeholders that have mutual goals to gather together, which would not be possible without such a partnership agreement.

Development banks, which are among the most important LTInv, are key actors at this level. They operate at regional, national, or supranational levels and can also be set up through different models of public-private governance. Their main role is to design and offer blending finance mechanisms, aimed at attracting (or crowding in) traditional investors to riskier investments, such as those related to the achievement of the SDGs. They are also crucial in defining standards and in supporting governments in the creation of a favorable ecosystem to develop LTIs. With specific regard to low- and middle-income countries, all the regional development banks, along with the International Finance Corporation and the World Bank, issued in 2015 a Development Committee Paper, "From Billions to Trillions: Transforming Development Finance," in which they highlighted the need to shift focus from "billions" in official development assistance to "trillions" in investments of all kinds to achieve the SDGs. This paper laid out an approach that asked multilateral development banks to enhance their financial leverage, ramp up assistance for domestic resource mobilization and efficient public spending, and catalyze private investment – also improving coordination and alignment. Based on the Addis Ababa Agenda for Action,[2] the World Bank Group has embarked on an effort to help countries maximize finance for development, and to do so responsibly without pushing the public sector into unsustainable levels of debt and contingent liabilities. This entails pursuing private-sector solutions where they can help achieve development goals and reserving scarce public finance for where it is most needed (World Bank, 2017).

These commitments are at the basis of a "paradigm shift on how development is and will be financed, to unlock the resources needed to achieve the SDGs. Indeed, the world needs intelligent development finance that goes well beyond filling financing gaps and that can be used strategically to unlock, leverage, and catalyze private flows and domestic resources" (World Bank, 2015).

Blended finance schemes, generally, based on tranching mechanisms (where public and impact investors invest in riskier layers to crowd in traditional institutional investors that take lower risk layers), are the cornerstone of the private capital mobilization for the achievement of the SDGs. They are forms of financial partnership at the meso level, which further down at the project level can also foster public-private co-investments. Forms of blending money at the meso level support infrastructure projects, that are also developed through concession contracts and include also public-private venture capital programs and guarantee programs. The former blend public and private money in order to increase the availability of equity capital to start-ups (as the main drivers of innovation, also societal); the latter provide collateral to support small and medium-sized enterprises to get access to debt. Blended finance mechanisms, and more specifically public-private funds, promote financial and economic additionality and are salient in the framework of public value creation.

At the micro level, PPP mainly happen through contracts between a public authority (a contracting authority – CA) and an economic operator (EO, single or in pool), profit or not for profit. Such contracts can take the form of a procurement contract, used by the authority to buy goods, services, or works from an EO, or a concession contract. The latter has a mid-/long-term horizon and allocates risk between the CA and the EO, in order to create incentives to achieve complex and/or innovative goals, which are more difficult to achieve through a traditional public procurement contract. The objective of such contracts is usually the delivery of a service or the development and operation of infrastructure where the EO is paid based on the results achieved, according to different contract schemes. To put it concisely, such payments can be either in the form of tariffs from end users (when the EO retains the demand risk) or availability charges, paid by the CA in return for a non-core service. In this instance, CAs retain full responsibility for the delivery of the main, or core, service. In recent years, outcome-based PPP contracts, also known as social impact bonds, have emerged; here, a premium is paid to EOs in proportion to the social result/outcome achieved.

The micro-level collaborations, by involving private players and local institutions through a strategic approach, allow for the achievement of a twofold goal. By acting as sophisticated buyer, the authority can improve public services and, at the same time, stimulate the market towards innovation, productivity, efficiency, and alignment to certain strategic goals such as innovation and sustainability. For instance, the inclusion of environmental and social goals in public contracts is becoming an increasingly common approach, since procurement is becoming a policy strategy instrument.

Figure 1.2 shows how macro, meso, and micro partnerships can be used by governments and public-sector actors to implement LTIs, by partnering, with different approaches and tools, with market players and investors. Some of these forms of collaboration are the focus of the next chapters.

Chapter 2 is dedicated to an analysis of the market trends towards a more sustainable economy, by shedding light on CSR and sustainable finance. Chapter 3 expands on a specific form of investment that strives to maximize the achievement of societal impact; it is dedicated to impact investing, which is analyzed both from the supply-side perspective (the investment approach) and from a demand-side perspective (the new emerging business models that embody the co-achievement of financial and societal return). Chapter 4 is dedicated to blended finance mechanisms, to mobilize more capital to sustain LTIs and the achievement of public value, with a focus on public-private venture capital funds and guarantees. Chapters 5 and 6 are dedicated to one of the most

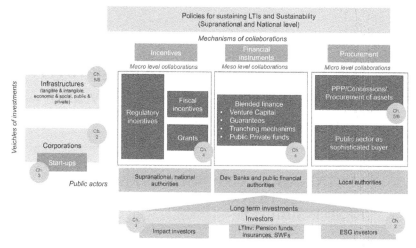

Figure 1.2   Public-private partnerships to activate long-term investments

important LTIs to achieve the SDGs, infrastructure; Chapter 5 discusses the main infrastructure delivery models in order to understand the rationale and boundaries of PPP contracts, which are analyzed in Chapter 6.

It is worth saying that the following chapters will discuss partnership mechanisms under a methodological perspective, with some references to relevant incidents and cases sourced from emerging and mature economies, used mainly to explain mechanisms. Therefore they do not have to be considered as best practices or exemplars.

NOTES

1. World Wealth Report, https://worldwealthreport.com, accessed March 11, 2022. High-net-worth individuals are defined as those having investable assets of USD 1 million or more, excluding primary residence, collectibles, consumables, and consumer durables.
2. The Action Agenda, adopted at the Third International Conference on Financing for Development (Addis Ababa, Ethiopia, July 2015) and endorsed by the General Assembly in its resolution 69/313 of July, 27, 2015, establishes a strong foundation to support the implementation of the 2030 Agenda for Sustainable Development. It provides a new global framework for financing sustainable development by aligning all financing flows and policies with economic, social, and environmental priorities.

2. The journey towards sustainability: corporate social responsibility and sustainable investing

1. SUSTAINABLE CORPORATE STRATEGIES: THE EVOLUTION OF CORPORATE SOCIAL RESPONSIBILITY

Sustainability, society, impact, responsibility, value creation, and public value are all terms that are now recurrent and dominant in the design of new corporate strategies and investment selection. When looking at the corporate side, many theories, constructs, concepts, and definitions have certainly come to bloom.

In the beginning, there was CSR. As reported by Carroll (1999), CSR was first introduced by Bowen in 1953, who can be considered the father of CSR. "[Bowen] refers to the obligations of businessmen to pursue those policies, to make those decisions, or to follow those lines of action which are desirable in terms of the objectives and values of our society" (p. 6). Bowen quoted Fortune Magazine's survey, wherein the magazine's editors thought that CSR, or the "social consciousness" of managers, meant that businessmen were responsible for the consequences of their actions in a sphere somewhat wider than that covered by their profit-and-loss statements (cited in Bowen, 1953, p. 44). "It is fascinating to note that 93.5 percent of the businessmen responding agreed with the statement" (Carroll, 1999).

In the same vein, despite not being famous at the global level, Bocconi University Professor Gino Zappa, who is considered the founder of the so-called "Economia Aziendale," the business administration discipline in Italy, in 1956 defined an enterprise as "an organisation that achieves with a long term view the satisfaction of human needs" (Zappa, 1957, p. 37).

It is now captivating to read such words, even though from the perspective we have today it is clear that the majority of the business world chose an entirely different direction. Otherwise, we would not have welcomed with such enthusiasm corporate sustainability proclamations, reports, or statements of commitment.

Later, Ed Freeman (1984) introduced the stakeholder theory, John Elkington (1994) the "triple bottom line," Rosabeth Moss Kanter (1999) "social innovation," Jed Emerson (2000) "blended value," and Michael Porter and Mark Kramer "shared value creation" (2011), which seems an expanded narrative of Drucker's words in 1984: "the proper 'social responsibility' of business is to tame the dragon, that is to turn a social problem into economic opportunity and economic benefit."

Despite the different terminologies, e.g., corporate citizenship, sustainability, stakeholder management, business ethics, shared value creation (SVC), conscious capitalism, and others, Carroll's four-part definition of CSR continues to be a relevant framework to delineate business responsibilities to the society of which they play a part (Carroll, 1979). He defines CSR as:

1. the economic responsibility to be profitable;
2. the legal responsibility to obey the law and comply with regulations;
3. the ethical responsibility to do what is right, just, and fair and to avoid or minimize harm to all the stakeholders with whom it interacts; and
4. discretionary philanthropic responsibility to be a good corporate citizen, that is, to give back and to contribute financial, physical, and human resources to the communities of which it is a part.

Carroll (1991) represented these four elements in the famous CSR pyramid where the first element is its foundation. In the words of Carroll (2016), "the pyramid should be seen as sustainable in that these responsibilities represent long term obligations that overarch into future generations of stakeholders."

The conceptualization of SVC by Porter and Kramer (2011) as an evolution of the social dimension of competitive context (Porter & Kramer, 2006) was heralded in the pages of the Harvard Business Review and it soon became popular.

SVC proposes to transform social problems relevant to the corporation into business opportunities, thereby contributing to solving critical societal challenges while simultaneously driving greater profitability. In the words of Porter and Kramer (2011, p. 65), SVC "can give rise to the next major transformation of business thinking," "drive the next wave of innovation and productivity growth in the global economy," and "reshape capitalism and its relationship to society."

Crane et al. (2014) offered a contrastive analysis of SVC. They highlighted that differently to others that "have presented corporate responsibility with regards to social and environmental problems as an ethical duty, a political responsibility, or a response to business risks," the strength of SVC stands in "invit[ing] corporations to perceive such problems not as disconnected and externally imposed but as real opportunities and serious strategic targets for genuine business decisions." A second value of SVC is represented by the clear role given to states in constructing "regulations that enhance shared value, set goals, and stimulate innovation." A third relevant strength is that SVC offers a holistic framework to reconcile different constructs such as CSR, non-market strategy, social entrepreneurship, social innovation, and the bottom of the pyramid, as well as to re-embed capitalism in society. However, they also noted that SVC is largely inspired by Ed Freeman's stakeholder theory (creating value for stakeholders creates value for shareholders); by Emerson's "blended value" concept (according to which firms seek simultaneously to pursue profit and social and environmental targets); by Hart's Capitalism at the Crossroads (2005); and by Moss Kanter's studies on "social innovation." Another weakness of SVC is the idea that "the purpose of the firm must be redefined" is wired, because what Porter and Kramer offered with their examples is largely confined to specific projects and products rather than the entire firm (Crane et al., 2014). Porter and Kramer replied to the critiques (2014) by saying, in a nutshell, that "using the profit motive and the tools of corporate strategy to address societal problems, a practice that is growing rapidly in part motivated by the shared value concept, can contribute greatly both to the redemption of business and to a better world."

We report this debate to underline the still contested nature of CSR. An interesting perspective of the evolution of CSR is offered by Visser (2011). In his view CSR 1.0 was focused on philanthropy, community relations, image building, and CSR departments (Visser, 2011, p. 144). CSR 2.0 differs from CSR 1.0 by shifting the focus from image to performance; from specialization to integration; from standardization to diversification; from Western to Global (Visser, 2011, p. 148). Such shifts have also been agreed by Carroll (2021). The founding pillars of CSR 2.0 are value creation, strong governance, societal/stakeholder contributions, and environmental integrity with sustainable ecosystems (2021, p. 150). Munro (2020) offered a further approach with "purpose" as an essential priority for corporations; innovation, inclusion, and collaboration with all partners; identification, engagement, and co-creation with all stakeholders; shared and integrated value at a deeper level; and measurable SDGs with ongoing assessment.

A contemporary shared view is that CSR initiatives must go "beyond good intentions" to achieve greater social impact (Barnett et al., 2020). In the words of Carroll (2021), the updated CSR trajectory might now look like this: CSR → corporate social responsiveness → corporate social performance → corporate social impact. Figure 2.1 shows a timeline of the evolution of CSR.

Leaving aside the words of scholars, the shift towards a new approach to society (and public value) can be captured in some of the most quoted statements.

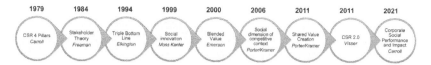

Figure 2.1   The evolution of corporate social responsibility

In August 2019, the Business Roundtable, the prestigious organization composed of chief executive officers (CEOs) of major corporations, announced an updated statement that posited a shift from shareholder primacy to a commitment to all stakeholders. Jamie Dimon (2020), Chairman and CEO of JPMorgan Chase and Chair of the Business Roundtable, believed that capitalism could be saved by business and government collaborating better to create opportunities for all.

Later, in August 2020, in a historic letter, a new coalition of global corporate leaders representing a combined annual revenue of over USD 100 billion and a combined global workforce of over 500,000 proposed a roadmap to "build the economic system better," rather than simply "building it back." The roadmap's goal was to create an inclusive and sustainable post-Covid-19 economy that benefits society, the planet, and shareholders, for generations to come. In the letter, the group of 14 CEOs called on governments to accelerate such a transition by recognizing and supporting purpose-first business as an emerging fourth sector of the economy.

Will it bring about real change? According to Bebchuk and Tallarita (forthcoming), business leader statements were "mostly for show" and Business Roundtable companies joining it did not intend or expect it to bring about any material changes in how they treat their stakeholders. Their findings support an emerging view that pledges by corporate leaders to serve stakeholders would not materially benefit stakeholders, and that their main effect could be to insulate corporate leaders from shareholder oversight and reduce pressures of regulators. The authors also believe that stakeholder governance that relies on the discretion of corporate leaders may not represent an effective way to address growing concerns about the effects that corporations have on stakeholders.

This further recalls the idea that more collaboration is needed to achieve real change in the way in which corporations behave.

2.   SUSTAINABLE INVESTING: THE PROGRESS AND CHALLENGES OF ESG INVESTING

Societal and environmental impacts are becoming increasingly relevant also for investors since they realize that ignoring such issues may harm long-term returns of the companies they own. Larry Fink (2020), CEO of BlackRock, the largest asset management company worldwide, stated his intention to exit certain investments that "present a high sustainability-related risk."

Other investors go beyond the risk management approach and ask for a better balance between social and financial returns advocating a new investment approach, which takes the name of impact investing (II), crafted in 2007 by Rockefeller Foundation, to refer to an investment approach made with the intention of generating financial return, including social and/or environmental impact. II is analyzed more in depth in Chapter 3.

Nowadays, according to the Global Impact Investing Network, II is no longer a market for just a few patient investors, among them foundations and philanthropists; indeed, asset management companies are now playing a pivotal role by bridging the sources of capital and investment opportunities. This critical role has come to enable asset owners to deploy capital towards today's social and environmental challenges more efficiently and effectively than they could have ever done otherwise. In the words of the Rockefeller Foundation, they "are bringing to the table something the traditional II community has thus far lacked: scale."

Next to growth in "pure" II, we are also seeing a dramatic surge of ESG investing, with almost USD 31 trillion in assets currently under management (Bloomberg Intelligence, 2021). According to analysts, by 2025 ESG investments should reach USD 53 trillion, also under a new policy framework, such as the European Union (EU) Green Deal. A report by the Carbon Disclosure Project (2019) highlights that the potential value of sustainable business opportunities could exceed seven times the cost of realizing them (USD 311 billion in costs against USD 2.1 trillion in opportunities).

In this landscape, boundaries between socially responsible investing (SRI), ESG investing and II are becoming blurred, and this is due to the fact that they suffer from a lack of clear definition, which poses challenges for their development (see Box 2.1 for a classification of the different approaches to sustainable investing). In particular, the risk perceived by pioneer ESG, impact investors, and asset managers is so-called "impact washing," or "greenwashing,"[1] which may also be the consequence of the fact that, despite the sophistication of impact measurement and management practices, a vast amount of urgent work is still needed. With the rapid growth of the market, questions can be and indeed have been raised. Is ESG just a tag, an advertising gimmick, or reality? What really does differentiate II from ESG investing? Concerns are mounting and the next few years will be crucial for the development/improvement of regulation and measurement frameworks.

BOX 2.1   A CLASSIFICATION OF APPROACHES TO SUSTAINABLE INVESTING

The recent developments in sustainable investing suffer from a heterogeneity of terminology in academic literature, as well as in public and private discourse. Terms such as SRI, ESG, and II are typical but are still used with generic and interchangeable meaning to refer to a wide set of investment approaches intended to generate some sort of impact on people and the planet.

Leveraging the spectrum of capital by Bridges Fund Management and mapping realized by the Impact Management Project, we provide a classification of sustainable investing approaches which encompass a broad range of risk/return strategies. In particular, we consider SRI, ESG, and II as different strategies that investors adopt, depending on their desired risk, return, and impact profile. Depending on their motivation, investors' intentions range from broad commitments, such as "to mitigate risk," "to avoid harm," "to achieve sustainable long-term financial performance," or "to leave a positive mark on the world," to more detailed objectives such as "to support a specific group of people, place, outcome" or "to address a specific social or environmental challenge."

As shown in Figure 2.2, these strategies fit into an investment continuum. Traditional investments lie on the left of this continuum and traditional philanthropy on the right. Over recent decades, impact-motivated investors have started to move towards the right, incorporating society and environment into their investment decisions. SRI applies a negative screen over harmful products (e.g., alcohol, tobacco, firearms, fossil fuels) and may also include consideration of a broader range of factors from a risk management perspective (e.g., use of child labor, sweatshops, pollution). ESG investing, which takes impact considerations to the next level, applies a positive screen, selecting investments based on proactive, positive E, S, and G factors (e.g., investing in firms proactively upskilling their employees, or selling products that support good health or educational outcomes). II aims to achieve intended social and environmental impact, and it requires measuring and reporting against this, demonstrating the intentionality of the investor and underlying asset/investee, as well as investor contribution. II targets highest-impact opportunities, which directly address issues and markets where a social or environmental need creates a business opportunity. As we will discuss in Chapter 3, we observe different risk/return strategies even within II, which are usually referred to as "finance-first" or "thematic" II, as opposed to "impact-first" II. While finance-first II generates targeted, direct impact while producing alpha (i.e., returns that are in line, or above, the market return), impact-first II provides patient capital, prioritizes impact objectives, and accepts below-market returns or just capital preservation.

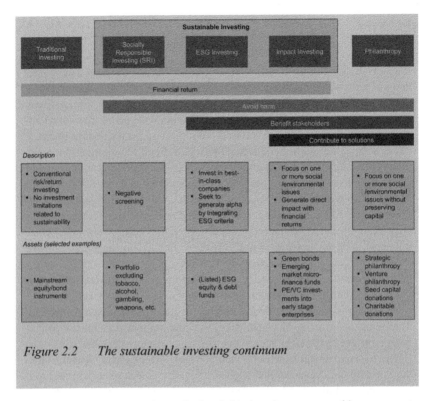

Figure 2.2   The sustainable investing continuum

Many ESG rating agencies and other initiatives have emerged in response to this rising popularity of ESG investing. Investors use ESG ratings (provided, for example, by agencies such as MSCI, Thomson Reuters, and Sustainalytics) and ESG indices (such as DJSI and FSTE4Good) as they provide a quick approximation of a firm's ESG quality. Scalet and Kelly (2010) defined an ESG rating agency/data providers as: "Any organization that rates or assesses corporations according to a standard of social and environmental performance that is at least in part based on non-financial data." Similar to ratings, indices serve as a framework for investment products and as benchmarks for assessing investment performance (Grayson & Nelson, 2013). These indices are often built on ESG ratings and even awards and rankings are regularly based on these scores (Mooij, 2017).

As reported by Mooij (2017), besides many ESG ratings, there are about 500 rankings, 170 different ESG-related indices, 100+ awards, and at least 120 voluntary standards. Furthermore, there are think tanks, institutions, and other associations with their own interpretation of how to tackle this area of concern (Vandekerckhove et al., 2012).

Domino 400, the first social investment benchmark, was launched in 1990. In the early 1990s, there were fewer than 20 publicly listed companies that issued reports that included ESG data. The number of publicly listed companies reporting ESG data has grown exponentially over the last two decades. As of 2020, 80 percent of the largest 100 companies in each of the 52 countries analyzed by KPMG (80 percent of 5,200 companies) issued sustainability reports with ESG data, a marked increase from the 12 percent in 1993; and among the world's 250 largest companies, the underlying trend for third-party assurance of sustainability data is 71 percent. Disclosure mainly follows sustainability-reporting guidelines and standards issued by the Global Reporting Initiative (an independent, international organization that helps businesses and other organizations take responsibility for their impact, by providing them with a global common language to communicate the impact – launched in 2016), followed by the use of those issued by the Sustainability Accounting Standards Board and International Standards Organization (KPMG, 2020).

This growing salience of ESG is not unique to corporations but it is also becoming prevalent in the asset management industry. For example, United Nations Principle for Responsible Investments was launched in 2006 at the New York Stock Exchange, after the 2005 call of the then United Nations Secretary-General Kofi Annan to a group of the world's largest institutional investors. Since then, the number of signatories has grown from 100 to over 4,000.

Many scholars and experts have found and documented that ESG ratings, benchmarks, and stock indices are often imprecise: they rely on scarce or incomplete and sometimes conflicting data (Tirole, 2017) and provide only limited information on material ESG factors (Schoenmaker & Schramade, 2019), which are those that drive performance (Khan et al., 2016). This is because they are based on reported data and policies provided by companies, where larger ones can rely on bigger budgets and teams. As noted by Mooij (2017) "ratings are not necessarily intended to increase shareholder value and … it is indeed often simply a tick the box exercise."

Therefore, it is not surprising to see a lack of correlation in scores between rating agencies. Across 1,600 stocks in the MSCI World benchmark, Howard (2016) finds a correlation of 26 percent between the scores assigned by the two largest rating agencies. Based on survey data, Mooij (2017) concluded that "reporting fatigue, a lack of convergence and the (sometimes) poor quality and transparency have made the ESG rating industry more vice than virtue in the adoption of responsible investment." In the same vein, a Wall Street Journal article noted that "Environmental, social and governance criteria are hard to define. When we measure how different ESG providers rate companies in the S&P 500, there's often little overlap. By contrast, when rating agencies score those same companies for their creditworthiness, they are much more often in agreement" (Sindreu & Kent, 2018).

In contrast to other contexts, where greater disclosure helps reduce disagreement among information intermediaries, Chistensen et al. (2021) found that greater ESG disclosure leads to greater ESG disagreement across ESG rating agencies, at least with reference to environmental and social data, rather than that relating to governance.

Further to these critiques, ESG scores are "industry neutral" and based mainly on operations, without considering products of the companies under assessment and, more in general, the impact on the environment and society. As Schoenmaker and Schramade (2019) argued this can result in ratings that are biased if not wrong, as the least bad companies in very unsustainable industries (e.g., coal or tobacco) can get remarkably high scores and can be considered leaders in sustainability.

Quantitative metrics are used mainly with reference to the E dimension of ESG, with many companies now reporting their scope 1, 2, and 3 carbon dioxide emissions[2] following the adoption of the Greenhouse Gas Protocol; on the S dimension, quantitative metrics are used with reference to the percentage of women on the workforce, job creation, and safety data; on the G side, the number of independent directors, gender balance, and voting rules are considered. As noted by Schoenmaker and Schramade (2019) it is certainly encouraging to see that these data are provided and analyzed, but "there are also limitations to analysing the performance on specific KPIs [key performance indicators]," because they are too narrow and context specific, while the sustainability issue is a more holistic concept, as discussed above with reference to the debate on CSR. Furthermore, it is difficult to relate these punctual metrics with contributions to the SDGs, both in terms of specific company and in terms of industry. Actually, a KPMG report (2020) highlights that a significant majority of companies (86 percent among 5,200 and 90 percent of the world's 250 largest) report a one-sided view focused only on their positive SDG impact.

However, frameworks are emerging to support companies moving from measuring to outcomes (such as product outcome), which are also better able to link to the SDGs.

In the majority of cases companies report on environmental or social externalities related to operations (input and processes/activities) and therefore they report on water consumption, waste generation, carbon emissions, employee health and safety records, or diversity and inclusion efforts. As Serafeim and Trinh (2020) noted, progress on measuring the impact that products have on consumers and society has been less impressive (product impact metrics).

Further to this, as reported by the KPMG report (2020), environmental and social metrics are not yet embedded in a financial statement framework (so-called integrated reporting, combining both financial and non-financial data in a single annual report) to illustrate their value implications and to enable managers and investors to understand trade-offs and relative performance evaluation that considers impact along with risk and return (Serafeim & Trinh, 2020).

"Investors lack transparency on the impact companies make through their products, employment and operations," Sir Ronald Cohen wrote in July 2020 in the *Financial Times*. In another interview in the *Financial Times* published in August 2021, he said:

> If governments force companies to publish impact-weighted accounts (e.g., integrated reports with a monetization of positive and negative externalities), they will immediately start to focus on improving their impact and finding solutions to social and environmental problems ... If we continue with a system of just reporting impact in general terms, investors won't have the means of assuring that they optimize return and impact. That's why I have been pushing very hard for impact accounting to become mandatory.[3]

The Harvard Business School Impact Weighted Accounts Initiative, chaired by Sir Ronald Cohen, found 56 companies that have experimented with monetary impact valuation, producing environmental or total profit and loss accounts. Of these, 86 percent are measuring environmental impact, 50 percent are estimating employment/social impact, but only 20 percent are estimating product impact. Impact-weighted accounts would ease the flow of accurate information for a more efficient allocation of ESG assets (Serafeim et al., 2019).

Many scholars and experts have also pointed out the very great need of a higher level of engagement of investors with investee companies (Schoenmaker & Schramade, 2019), which is something that already happens in the II domain.

Porter et al. (2019) noted that "creating shared value is fundamentally distinct from making incremental improvements in a long checklist of ESG factors that tend to converge over time in any given industry." Drawing on such concerns, it must be noted that a plethora of things are currently happening in the domain of ESG reporting with the intent to formulate a more comprehensive and coherent corporate reporting system.

The five leading voluntary framework and standard setters – Carbon Disclosure Project (CDP), Climate Disclosure Standards Board (CDSB), Global Reporting Initiative (GRI), International Integrated Reporting Council (IIRC), and Sustainability Accounting Standards Board (SASB) – have for the first time committed to work towards a joint vision. The International Integrated Reporting Council and the Sustainability Accounting Standards Board have also merged to form the Value Reporting Foundation.

At the 2020 Annual Meeting in Davos, 120 of the world's largest companies, under the umbrella of the International Business Council, in collaboration with Deloitte, EY, KPMG, and PwC, presented a set of universal, material ESG metrics and recommended disclosures that could be reflected in mainstream annual reports on a consistent basis across industry, sectors, and countries. The primary focus of this initiative was to encourage as many companies as possible to start reporting on the recommended core metrics in mainstream annual reports and disclosures. With this goal, the initiative has scanned the many hundreds of ESG metrics available and highlighted just 21 core metrics that are well established, universal, industry agnostic, and that appear to be material to sustainable value creation (World Economic Forum, 2020). Furthermore, they identified 34 expanded metrics to encourage companies to move from reporting outputs alone to capturing the impact of their operations, especially on nature and society across the full value chain, in more tangible, sophisticated ways – including the monetary value of impact. The metrics have been organized into four pillars – principles of governance, planet, people, and prosperity – which are aligned with the essential elements of the SDGs.

On the institutional side, the United States (US) Securities and Exchange Commission amended its business disclosure rules in August 2020 to enhance the focus on human capital disclosures, which "can be an important driver of long-term value," according to its Chairman Jay Clayton.[4]

The leading institution in this landscape is certainly the European Commission. In April 2021, it adopted a proposal for a Corporate Sustainability Reporting Directive, which would amend the existing reporting requirements of the Non-Financial Reporting Directive. It represented a bold piece of legal framework, along with the Climate Benchmarks Regulation (which came into force in December 2020), the Sustainable Finance Disclosure Regulation (which came into force in March 2021), and the Taxonomy Regulation (which came into force in July 2020), creating the world's first ever "green list" – a classification system for environmentally sustainable economic activities. While the Taxonomy Regulation focuses on environmental indicators, the more recent Sustainable Finance Disclosure Regulation creates a broader transparency framework for European sustainable investment products, by introducing a catalogue of mandatory and voluntary indicators in relation to the climate and environment, as well as to social and employee matters, respect for human rights, anti-corruption, and anti-bribery matters. The overall EU package is aimed at creating a consistent and coherent flow of sustainability information throughout the financial value chain as an essential part of the European Green Deal and a condition to avoid greenwashing, and therefore to ensure Europe is climate neutral by 2050 (EU Commission, 2021). As we will discuss further, the European Commission is starting to apply the taxonomy also to public investments.

As Sir Cohen said in his 2021 interview with the *Financial Times*, if "bringing impact into investment decisions and the success for business is redefined as maximum profit with maximum impact, then you can see how business and investors can bring solutions to our problems instead of aggravating them."

3. THE JOURNEY TOWARDS SUSTAINABILITY IN THE PUBLIC SECTOR

In this context, we may ask ourselves what role the public sector is playing and how the trends that have just been described intersect with public policies, strategies, and operations. Though contested, fragmented, and still in evolution, the progress towards sustainability under way in the private sector is not only massive and broad but, as shown in previous paragraphs, at the core of the debate in professional and institutional roundtables, as well as being reported on, on almost a daily basis, by major media channels. Are private-sector efforts the result of public action, and do they just anticipate policies soon to be enacted? Or do they actually contribute to setting the agenda pushing governments to react? To put it differently, are companies just lobbying, acting as corporate citizens, or is society really recognized as a source of a new competitive advantage? Recognizing the role of the private sector in solving global issues not only assumes that it is part of the problem and has a duty in trying to address it, but also provides an indirect measure of the perceived failure of public institutions to address those same challenges.

Governments across the world are responsible, of course, for setting policies. With regards to the environment, since the Earth Summit in Rio de Janeiro in 1992, followed by the Kyoto Protocol in 1997 which led to the Paris Agreement in 2015, governments have set goals and strategies in order to try to tackle climate change. The Millennium Development Goals adopted in 2000 and SDGs adopted in 2015 have contributed to further popularizing the concept of sustainable development. At the policy level, supranational institutions have made salient progress to create frameworks, like the SDGs, to measure sustainability and set challenging goals for the private sector, or to define ambitious investment programs to channel public and private resources into achieving development goals. Regulations across the world are setting tougher environmental and labor standards.

However, when looking at the public sector's own operations and managerial practices, the impression is of a slower embrace compared to their private counterpart, which is at odds with the intrinsic role of government. It is true that government organizations do not produce technically designed and manufactured products, but rather deliver intangible services, which implies a small environmental impact. For example, in developed economies like the EU and US, the public sector[5] in 2020 was responsible for about 20 percent of total value added but accounted for 4 percent of domestic energy use only. If the environmental dimension is less relevant in a productive perspective, public organizations should be trailblazers with flagship projects. With regards to other relevant dimensions, the public sector is a big employer (about 20 percent of total employment in Organisation for Co-operation and Development (OECD) countries in 2019) and consumer of resources (public procurement accounted for 12.6 percent of gross domestic product in OECD countries in 2019) (OECD, 2021a); this should dictate an important role in achieving sustainable development. When referring to investments, the public sector in major economies (US, EU, China) accounts for around 15 percent of total gross fixed capital formation; therefore, the inclusion of the sustainability dimension in investment decisions and operations is crucial.

The most common practices adopted by public agencies are environmental performance evaluation, audits, reporting, good practice awards, ecolabeling, and green public procurement (Figueira et al., 2018). However, the public sector still lacks an agreed framework for measuring and reporting sustainable practices; public green procurement is often limited to the adoption of basic environmental codified standards; and public employee motivation rarely leverages on bold sustainability policies, as happens in the private sector. As per the debate emerging in the private sector, and the holistic nature of sustainability, an integrative "portfolio" of policies and practices is required, whilst urging for the public sector to incorporate sustainability within its strategy. In doing so, it is important to consider not only the typical practices adopted by the private sector, especially with reference to the E and S dimensions of ESG, but also, and foremost, the G dimension.

One of the main obstacles in embedding sustainability in the action of public organizations lies, according to Osborne et al. (2014), in the new public management theory, which encouraged change by adopting business-like practices but as a side effect encouraged a short-term and transactional approach to the delivery of public services. Indeed, the authors recommend to embrace the New Public Governance paradigm. Government has to engage, promote, and coordinate efforts by private and not-for-profit stakeholders to reach common goals (sustainability is indeed a common goal). In the context of administrative rigidity and lack of competence, to face unanticipated opportunities and difficulties posed by climate change, for instance, it is urgent to better integrate the efforts made by governments as regulators and as market players (public-sector organizations as service providers) and engage, promote, and coordinate efforts from private and not-for-profit stakeholders to foster sustainable development (Koppenjan & Enserink, 2009).

In this sense PPP contracts and public procurement are powerful instruments for translating these theoretical concepts into concrete action because they can not only improve the inner sustainability of the public sector (i.e., by purchasing less-polluting goods or by achieving higher social outcomes), but also to stimulate business to generate SDG-consistent solutions and therefore become more innovative. It is not only a matter of applying social or environmental standards, as it has been until now, but of radically changing the way goods, services, and infrastructure are designed. One step in this direction is the introduction, by the European Commission, of the "do no significant harm principle," set out by the EU taxonomy for sustainable activities to be applied to all investments financed by the recovery and resilience facility and structural funds. This is a novel approach since it treats public and private investments in the same way and forces public authorities to integrate sustainability in the way they conceive and enact their investments. From a managerial point of view, if the public sector is called to act as a sophisticated buyer, asking for innovative solutions, pushing the boundaries of what is technically and economically achievable, businesses should also change tack and become sophisticated suppliers and strategic partners, and not only trusted providers.

The public sector has to seriously embrace sustainability at the organizational level, also as a way to reinforce policy efforts. It is not "sustainable" to ask (through regulation) the private sector to change if the change does not also happen in the public sector. Both sectors, in a coordinated manner, are salient to the achievement of a more sustainable society and economy. If in the private sector the main drivers towards sustainability are represented by regulation, shareholders, or even just a desire to imitate the approach, in the public sector there is no attempt to assist the application of such pressure, from either policymakers and/or even citizens.

NOTES

1.   See, for example, the Global Impact Investment Network 2020 Annual Impact Investor Survey.
2.   Scopes 1, 2, and 3 emissions are greenhouse gas emissions that cause carbon footprints. Scope 1 emissions are direct emissions from owned or controlled sources. Scope 2 emissions are indirect emissions from the generation of purchased energy. Scope 3 emissions are all indirect emissions (not included in Scope 2) that occur in the value chain of the reporting company, including both upstream and downstream emissions (Greenhouse Gas Protocol, www .ghgprotocol.org/sites/default/files/ghgp/standards_supporting/Diagram%20of %20scopes%20and%20emissions%20across%20the%20value%20chain.pdf).
3.   Sir Ronald Cohen on the Impact Accounting "Revolution," *Financial Times*, August 20, 2021, www.ft.com/content/bbca62ed-9e21-4f54-810c-4697852c30a2.
4.   www.sec.gov/news/press-release/2020-192.

5.		Here defined in statistical terms (NACE activity-sector codes) as public adminis-
		tration, defense, education, human health, and social work activities.

3. Catalyzing wealth to drive positive social and environmental change: impact investing

1. IMPACT INVESTING: MORE THAN A BUZZWORD

II has been one of the buzzwords of the decade. In 2007, the Rockefeller Foundation convened a meeting at the Bellagio Centre in Italy on philanthropy and developmental finance, where the term "impact investing" was used for the first time (Bugg-Levine & Goldstein, 2009). Although investment firms adopting an II-like approach such as Acumen Fund, Aavishkaar fund, and Bridges Fund Management have been operational since much earlier, II has only gained increased recognition over the past 15 years.

The market for II has been proliferating with different financial institutions, foundations, government agencies, and high-net-worth individuals (HNWIs) pooling capital, simultaneously in the pursuit of social and financial goals. The current size of the global II market is difficult to estimate, due to the lack of comprehensive analysis, the problematic access to quality information for all the actors in the II ecosystem, and, above all, different views on what is included in II. Boundaries between II and other sustainable investment strategies such as SRI and ESG are becoming blurred, therefore, market estimations and analysis suffer from a heterogeneity in II classification, which poses challenges for the development of the industry. Below are some estimations:

- The Global Impact Investing Network (GIIN) has been surveying a subset of the II market for the past ten years; in their latest global survey, they interviewed 294 II asset managers and organizations and estimated that the total amount globally committed to II was USD 715 billion in 2020, including more than 1,700 investors worldwide; 69 percent of respondents viewed the II market as "growing steadily."[1]
- The Global Sustainable investment Alliance estimated the II market at USD 352 billion in 2020, with a compound annual growth rate of 9 percent over the past five years.[2]

- The latest estimate by the International Finance Corporation, part of the World Bank Group, showed that USD 2.3 trillion was being invested for impact in 2020, corresponding to about 2 percent of global assets under management (AuM).[3]

Even if there is no consensus on the precise size of the II market, all the available statistics and analyses agree that II remains a niche market, but one that is attracting growing interest. In this scenario, several critical trends are coming together.

Firstly, in a context of global challenges such as the pressing environmental crisis, with increasing welfare impoverishment and infrastructure deficit, there is growing recognition that the existing set of resources allocated to address these issues is insufficient. The World Economic Forum estimates a persistent USD 2.5 trillion annual financing gap that stands in the way of achieving the SDGs by 2030.[4] Not only will II be key to funding the SDGs, but it will also play an important role in finding solutions to problems conventionally seen as the domain of the public sector, which is increasingly finding it difficult to cope with the more diversified needs of societies. For example, in welfare services, the aging population is projected to increase spending on pensions, healthcare, long-term care, education, and unemployment benefits by 14.2 percent by 2070 solely in the EU, creating a gap that cannot be covered with solutions and resources provided by the public sector alone.[5]

Secondly, a new generation of entrepreneurs with a social mission as well as a profit motive is growing, and more companies are set up to explicitly pursue sustainability strategies. Across the world, almost half of the people that are creating ventures have a social or environmental purpose compared to those with solely a commercial aim, according to the Global Entrepreneurship Monitor.[6]

At the same time, private investors, especially younger ones, believe investment can be used for good or for ill, and they are more and more committed to making investments with a positive social and environment impact. Despite the pandemic crisis, private wealth has never been higher at a global level. In 2020, private liquidity has risen by 7.6 percent, reaching a historical peak of USD 79.5 trillion.[7] Thanks to the low return rate from traditional asset classes, and the awareness and pushing agenda for sustainability, more and more investors see driving social and environmental impact as being something that is important; this trend is led by younger investors, under 40 years, and by those located in emerging markets.

II has been ranking high in the policy agenda of governments and international organizations, as well as in the strategies of global financial institutions. Among others, the G8 established a taskforce dedicated to II back in 2013, and the World Economic Forum runs a platform to integrate and aggregate best practices in this area. The EU, through the European Investment Bank (EIB) and its financial arm, the European Investment Fund (EIF), is pouring EUR 243 million into the development of the European market for II. In the US, the Small Business Administration has a dedicated facility of USD 1 billion to create licensed funds that target social and financial returns. Even large global investment banks, like JPMorgan and Citi Bank, have been the main promoters of this investment approach. These organizations, alongside the Rockefeller Foundation, the Omidyar Network, and others, are the main supporters of the GIIN, which has been operational for a decade, gathering more than 500 members and collecting statistics and best practices on the II market.

Despite its promises and the increasing garnered attention over recent years, the growth in the number of studies on II has been surprisingly low (see Agrawal & Hockerts, 2021), and someone new to the topic may be overwhelmed with overlapping concepts, from SRI and ESG investing to venture philanthropy. In Chapter 2 we provided a classification of the different approaches to sustainable investing, and we clarified that we consider SRI, ESG, and II as different strategies that investors adopt, depending on their desired risk, return, and impact profile, which fit into an investment continuum. In this chapter, we aim to deepen our understanding of II by explaining its key elements and scope, and critically discuss its current and future developments.

2.   IMPACT INVESTING AS AN INVESTMENT APPROACH

2.1   Distinguishing Features of Impact Investing

Definitions of II are numerous and evolving; however, the most commonly used definition is the one provided by GIIN: "II are investments made with the intention to generate positive, measurable social and environmental impact alongside a financial return." Based on this definition, II can be regarded as an investment strategy, within a broader range of sustainable investing risk/return strategies, which is characterized by three main distinguishing features (Brest & Born, 2013; Rodin & Brandenburg, 2014):

*   Intentionality in targeting specific social or environmental impact. Investor intention to address a specific social or environmental challenge through investment is at the core of II, therefore investments or investors supporting impactful business without specifically targeting impact should be disqualified from being regarded as II; this also marks the difference with ESG investing, where investments or investors aim to achieve sustainable long-term financial performance by integrating different environmental, social, and governance factors.

- Additionality of the social or environmental impact achieved. Investments increase the quantity or quality of the social or environmental outcome beyond what would otherwise have occurred; this poses challenges in terms of impact measurement, as II would require measurement and reporting against intended social or environmental impact, as well as demonstrating the investor contribution.
- Generation of financial return. Investors expect the return of capital (i.e., the reimbursement of their initial investment), plus some return on this capital, which may range from zero (in the case of just capital preservation) to market returns. This marks the difference between a philanthropic or venture philanthropic approach.

2.2   Risk/Return Strategies and Impact Objectives

II approaches adopted by investors vary in their risk/return expectations and impact objectives. To put it simply, they are usually divided into two groups: "finance-first" or "thematic" II, and "impact-first" II. Finance-first II generates targeted, direct impact while producing alpha (i.e., returns that are in line, or above the market return), and typically focuses on less challenging issues and lower-risk models. In contrast, impact-first II provides patient capital and prioritizes impact objectives by focusing on tougher issues and aiming to pilot new models; for these reasons, it often (but not always) targets below-market returns or accepts higher financial risk. In some cases, blended finance layered structures are applied in II (see Chapter 4 for a review of blended finance techniques and instruments), and some investors are willing to accept lower returns/higher risk in order to make the transaction attractive to more risk-adverse investors, such as mainstream LTInv, by leaving the higher-return/lower-risk tranches available to them and, therefore, catalyzing additional capital into impact opportunities.[8] According to GIIN, two out of three investors in the market target risk-adjusted market-rate returns, while only one out of three target below-market-rate returns. Figure 3.1 positions "finance-first" and "impact-first" II in the investment continuum presented in Chapter 2 based on the targeted financial and impact returns.

The generation of financial returns alongside social and environmental impact in II has long been debated, raising the question of the existence of a trade-off between social and financial returns. This idea has led to the misconception that social and environmental impact is always at the expense of financial return, which is not applicable, at least in II, which targets impact opportunities that directly address issues and markets where a social or environmental need creates a business opportunity. As we will discuss in Section 3 of this chapter, the alignment between an investee's ability to generate impact and their ability to deliver financial returns with a commercially viable

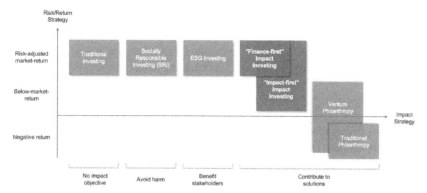

*Figure 3.1   Positioning impact investing based on the risk/return strategy
and impact objectives*

business model permits the scaling-up of operations and impact at a faster rate than happens in the traditional charity model, which is largely dependent upon annual fundraising.

While some II (similar to traditional ones) may have underperformed return expectations, today there is enough evidence to conclude that it is not necessary to sacrifice returns to generate impact. For example, a study conducted by GIIN and Cambridge Associate[9] found that 51 II funds adopting a private equity strategy returned a 6.9 percent gross annual internal rate of return, compared to a rate of 8.1 percent for the commercial universe, with larger II funds even outperforming the benchmark.

2.3   Investment Instruments

Just over ten years ago, JPMorgan and the Rockefeller Foundation published a report[10] claiming that II was an emerging asset class. Now, there is growing consensus in the market that II is better described as an investment approach that spans different asset classes. While the notion of II originated in private equity and debt, which still represent the largest portion of AuM invested globally, many other asset classes offer investors impact opportunities, such as:[11]

- Cash/cash equivalents, e.g., investment of cash assets (such as certificates of deposit or savings accounts) into community banks and local financial institutions that provide funding to social enterprises, affordable housing, or sustainable agriculture.
- Fixed income instruments, e.g., green bonds issued by governments, corporations, or multilateral development banks; investments in micro-finance loan/bond funds.

- Listed equity and debt, e.g., listed micro-finance institutions or community banks.
- Private equity and debt, e.g., debt and equity investments made directly into impact enterprises, or into investment funds that make debt and equity investments into impact enterprises operating in various regions, targeting a broad range of impact themes.
- Real assets, e.g., affordable housing, renewable energy infrastructure, sustainable transportation.
- Hybrid investments, e.g., social impact bonds (SIBs) and development impact bonds (DIBs).

Investors can practice II across asset classes and deploy their capital through II instruments based on their risk/return preferences and their impact objectives, as well as the contribution they want to make to their investees. Investors indeed can have a hands-off approach towards their investees, or they can engage actively, using their expertise, networks, and influence to improve the environmental/societal performance of their investees. Investors' active engagement is key to support investees at an early stage of development and can include a wide spectrum of approaches – from dialogue with companies, to investors taking board seats and using their own team or consultants to provide hands-on management support (as seen in traditional venture capital, see Vecchi et al., 2017b). Figure 3.2 provides a classification of II instruments based on an investor's "finance-first" versus "impact-first" strategies and hands-off versus hands-on contributions.

2.4   Impact Investors

In terms of investor types, II has attracted a wide variety of investors, both individual and institutional, including development finance institutions, private foundations, religious institutions, family offices, HNWIs, as well as mainstream LTInv such as pension funds and insurance companies.

In the early days, II was supported by a small number of foundations and philanthropists, as well as a few pioneer HNWIs and family offices, motivated by testing out this new investment approach to advance their core social and/or environmental goals, while maintaining or growing their overall endowment. Nowadays, according to GIIN, II is no longer a market for just a few patient investors; indeed, profit asset management companies manage more than 50 percent of AuM in the market, and they play a pivotal role in bridging the sources of capital and investment opportunities. This critical role has come to enable asset owners to deploy capital towards today's social and environmental challenges more efficiently and effectively than they could have done

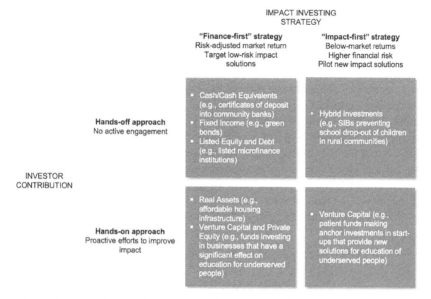

Figure 3.2   Financial instruments based on the investor's impact investment strategy and contribution

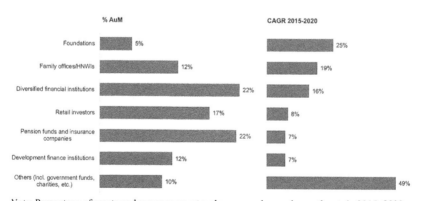

Note: Percentage of assets under management and compound annual growth rate in 2015–2020.
Source: Authors' elaboration, based on data from the Annual Impact Investor Survey, GIIN (2020).

Figure 3.3   Sources of capital in impact investing, by investor type

otherwise. In the words of the Rockefeller Foundation, they "are bringing to the table something the traditional II community has thus far lacked: scale."

As the industry has grown, asset managers report significantly increased investment into impact funds by foundations, family offices, and HNWIs, as described in Figure 3.3. Even if mainstream investors such as pension funds and insurance companies are still not the most active investors in II, they are increasingly considering II in their portfolio management strategy, providing more than 20 percent of AuM in the market. In this context, governmental agencies and development banks such as the Small Business Administration in the US and the EIB in Europe are supporting the development of the market, by sustaining the creation of dedicated asset managers, and making anchor investments to provide private asset owners with comfort and attract mainstream investors (see Box 3.1 for a review of the Social Impact Accelerator (SIA) initiative of the EIF, part of the EIB Group, to sustain the II market in Europe).

BOX 3.1   THE SOCIAL IMPACT ACCELERATOR MANAGED BY THE EUROPEAN INVESTMENT FUND

As part of a strategy to pioneer the II market and respond to a wider EU policy aim of establishing a funding market for innovative social entrepreneurship, the EIB Group set up the SIA facility, which reached its final closing in 2015 with an amount of EUR 243 million, combining resources from the EIB Group and external investors, including Credit Cooperatif and Deutsche Bank, as well as the Finnish group SITRA and the Bulgarian Development Bank.

SIA operates as a fund of funds managed by the EIF, providing capital to asset management companies and investing in venture capital funds which strategically target commercially viable social enterprises across Europe. According to the SIA definition, a "commercially viable social enterprise shall be a self-sustainable start-up whose business model serves to achieve a social impact. It shall provide an entrepreneurial solution to a societal issue based on a scalable approach and shall have a measurable impact." Beyond simple financial return targets, the funds backed by SIA are required to pursue explicit social or environmental impact targets at the level of their portfolio companies, by defining between one and five impact indicators per portfolio company and setting pre-investment quantifiable objectives for each of the indicators. In addition to impact targets, the target risk-adjusted internal rate of return required by SIA is between 3 and 5 percent, thus clearly excluding non-profitable investments from the scope of the facility.

With its configuration, SIA aims to build the market infrastructure for II in such a way that the market is placed on a path to long-term sustainability. Indeed, SIA does not invest directly into companies but supports the creation of dedicated asset managers and II funds by making anchor investments which attract other private asset owners. At the time of writing, SIA has invested approximately EUR 200 million in 17 funds, contributing to a collective fund capital of more than EUR 750 million.

3.   THE TARGETS OF IMPACT INVESTING

3.1   Categorizing Impact Investees: From Social to Societal Impact Enterprises

Impact investors can place their capital either directly or through financial intermediaries, such as asset management companies, as discussed above. As the ultimate target of investment, II invests in a broad range of enterprises (investees) targeting social or environmental impact with a sustainable business model. While investors can deploy their money across different asset classes, final II recipients usually receive capital in the form of debt and equity, or quasi-equity. Other sources of capital, such as grants and donations, are not considered forms of II.

Over recent decades, organizations pursuing a social or environmental mission while relying on a commercial business model have made the headlines. While the combination of financial sustainability and impact has been traditionally merged into the concept of social entrepreneurship (Dees, 1998; Austin et al., 2006; Peredo & McLean, 2006), innovative and commercially viable business models have paved the way to a new approach to achieving social and environmental impact while sustaining wealth creation (Santos et al., 2015). Below, we briefly discuss the evolution of social hybrid business models before providing a typology of the target investees of II.

Social entrepreneurship can be traced back to the early 1980s and originated in the social sector as a number of non-profits started to seek additional revenue by applying business expertise and managerial skills. Under a narrow perspective, social enterprises were defined as mission-driven organizations, where wealth creation was just a means to reach the desired impact (Dees, 1998; Thompson, 2002). These types of organization have been regarded as fragile and running the risk of internal tension and mission drift due to holding incompatible goals (Battilana & Dorado, 2010; Battilana & Lee, 2014; Doherty et al., 2014); furthermore, traditional social enterprises may find it difficult to achieve financial sustainability and reach scale (Santos, 2012). More recently, conventional sector boundaries have started to break down as societies search for more innovative, cost-effective, and financially sustainable ways to solve social and environmental problems. One result has been a rise in the number of entrepreneurs who want to combine a social purpose with a commercial organizational structure, aligning the activities that generate profit with the activities that generate impact (Dees & Anderson, 2003). Therefore, the distinction between social and commercial entrepreneurship is less and less dichotomous, but rather more accurately conceptualized as a continuum ranging from purely charitable to purely commercial business models. Between the two extremes, there are hybrid social business models that show elements of both. That is, there is significant heterogeneity in the types of organizational structure and business models that can fall under a broader social business rubric (Austin et al., 2007; Dees & Anderson, 2003).

In this context, leveraging the framework by Santos et al. (2015), we argue that these hybrid social business models are characterized by two dimensions, which are critical for the alignment between profit- and impact-generating activities in II target investees; these dimensions are *impact spillovers* and the *degree of overlap between clients and beneficiaries*.

Impact spillovers correspond to increases in the quantity or quality of a social or environmental outcome, which stem from either the production or consumption of goods or services delivered by an organization beyond what would otherwise have occurred; impact spillovers are more often called *positive externalities* in economic language. These impact spillovers lie at the heart of the concept of additionality in II, as we discussed above. In some situations, spillovers are *direct*, meaning that they happen automatically just by the fact of providing a product or service, while in other situations the impact spillovers are *contingent* on the development of additional intervention because they are not a direct outcome of activities. For example, the commercialization of solar rechargeable lanterns for low-income and rural communities creates significant direct impact spillovers in terms of reduction of carbon emissions by replacing the burning of kerosene, as well as improved educational outcomes due to better reading light for children to study. On the contrary, in micro finance, the provision of micro loans per se does not directly allow for the achievement of a social mission of poverty alleviation; micro-finance institutions need to target unbankable entrepreneurs and engage in significant mentoring activities with their clients to help them develop successful entrepreneurial activities and make the best use of their surplus income.

The *degree of overlap between clients and beneficiaries* is the alignment between those who pay for a product or service and those who benefit from it according to the social mission. The effectiveness of commercially viable models in delivering impact spillovers relies on consumers being willing and able to pay a price for a product or service that is above the cost of delivering it, allowing for value to be captured by both transacting parties. Excluded, disadvantaged, or low-income groups generally experience difficulties in accessing products or services generating impact spillovers due to their inability to pay; in these cases, third-party funders like governments and donors have traditionally incentivized the consumption of these goods, resulting in charitable models that provide free-of-charge or underpriced services. In these cases, where clients and beneficiaries are different groups, business models need to serve both groups, resulting in more complex structures that are harder to manage and scale. Innovative hybrid social business models, thanks to a redesign of the value chain aimed at lowering the costs and/or changing the offering system, make products and services more affordable and accessible, as well as aligning clients and target beneficiaries.

These two dimensions are the basis for classifying hybrid social business models, as shown in the matrix of Figure 3.4.

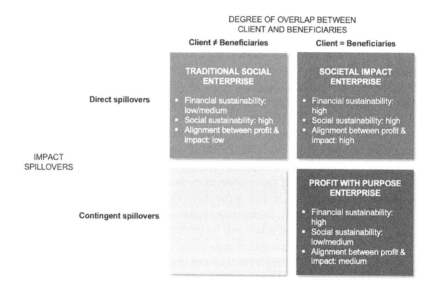

Figure 3.4   A classification of hybrid social business models

Among the different configurations of hybrid social business models, *societal impact enterprises* are mission-driven for-profit enterprises, where impact and financial sustainability are both part of the same business mission. They are the perfect target for II, as they address issues and markets where a social or environmental need creates a business opportunity, and their business model is designed in such a way that beneficiaries are clients that are willing and able to pay for a product or service for which the impact spillovers happen automatically. Examples include the Spanish company Sadako Technologies, which developed a solution combining computer vision, artificial intelligence capabilities, and robotics to optimize the amount of recoverable products in waste treatment plants and reduce the amount of waste that ends up in landfills, or Lifebank, a for-profit company based in Nigeria that, thanks to an innovative multimodal distribution platform, delivers critical medical supplies such as blood and oxygen faster, cheaper, and safer to hospitals and healthcare centers to the very last mile. These companies, given that the impact is directly derived from commercial activities, never pursue the social or environmental objectives at the expense of profitability. By focusing on the scaling-up of operations and commercial performance, societal impact enterprises simultaneously enhance their impact, therefore they are unlikely to experience mission drift.

Like societal impact enterprises, *profit-with-purpose enterprises* are organizations that serve paying clients who are also the beneficiaries of their societal mission, therefore they represent a possible target for II. However, for profit-with-purpose enterprises achieving the desired societal impact requires a specific focus on underserved social needs as well as additional interventions (such as training or community outreach) upon which positive impact spillovers are contingent. Profit-with-purpose enterprises include micro finance, or organizations that require changes in behavior on the part of clients for impact to happen. An example is the German start-up Company Bike, which partners with corporate clients to offer employees leasing bicycles and electric bikes made cheaper via salary conversion, which incentivizes commuting by bike through awareness campaigns about emissions and reduced urban congestion. Since profit-with-purpose enterprises may be exposed to a higher risk of mission drift, the boards of these companies should focus on monitoring the profile of clients served since their business model may lead them to prioritize clients with a higher ability to pay and neglect disadvantaged clients/beneficiaries who require the most additional interventions.

As a third type of hybrid social business model, *traditional social enterprises* serve clients and beneficiaries who are from different groups, offering a mix of free-of-charge and priced services. For these companies, self-sustainability is a vehicle to reach the social mission, and margins from operations, when generated, are reinvested. An example of a traditional social enterprise is San Patrignano, a community located in the center of Italy that welcomes those suffering from drug addiction and marginalization and helps them to find their way thanks to a rehabilitation program that is mainly based on vocational training. While the rehabilitation program is free of charge for beneficiaries and their families, financial suitability is reached thanks to clients buying the products (e.g., artisanal products, deli foods, etc.) produced by resident beneficiaries in their vocational training program. For such companies, the challenge of achieving financial sustainability is high, as the social mission requires focusing on the needs of beneficiaries and at the same time delivering a value proposition to the clients while operating in a competitive market.

In Figure 3.5, hybrid social business models are plotted in a continuum ranging from purely charitable to purely commercial business models and funding approaches. As shown in the continuum, societal impact enterprises are the typical target for II, as they combine profit and impact by addressing social or environmental needs with innovative solutions. While profit-with-purpose enterprises were excluded from II in the early days, with the growth of the industry, they have attracted more and more II capital, even if this requires demonstrating the additionality of the impact generated by the solution compared to already existing models, as we will discuss in Section 4. Traditional social enterprises are usually not the target of II, but instead they are the typical investees for venture philanthropy, where the approach includes both the use of reimbursable capital and grants. Boundaries among the different approaches are blurred and some impact-first investors could decide to support social enterprises that are 100 percent self-sustainable. However, it must be noted that traditional social enterprises and venture philanthropy cannot be part of a broader asset allocation strategy as they cannot reach scale through return-driven growth of assets, which is instead the aim of II (Grabenwarter & Liechtenstein, 2011).

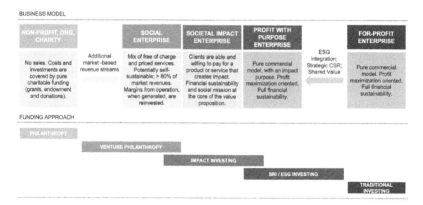

Figure 3.5   The business model and funding approach continuum

Besides purely private business models, which represent the majority of AuM invested globally, II can also target PPP projects to provide innovative welfare services through outcome-based contracts such as SIBs and DIBs. As we discuss in more depth in Box 3.2, impact investors can provide the capital to test and scale innovative service models, and governments repay those investors if and when the project achieves outcomes that generate social or environmental impact.

BOX 3.2   OUTCOME-BASED PUBLIC-PRIVATE PARTNERSHIP CONTRACTS AS ANOTHER TARGET OF IMPACT INVESTING

SIBs represent an additional investment target of II, which encompasses entering into a contract with the public sector. SIBs are indeed outcome-based PPP projects, with a contractual structure very similar to the availability-based contractual PPP model described in Chapter 6, aimed at financing and delivering welfare services instead of infrastructure. Launched for the first time in the United Kingdom (UK) in 2010 as a policy measure to reduce direct public intervention in social services, SIBs were conceived not only to overcome the typical shortcomings of traditional public and third-sector service provision (i.e., lack of capital, need for performance management, low efficiency, and low accountability), but also to bring more innovation to service design and delivery, and encourage key stakeholders to focus on the achievement of higher social outcomes. SIB applications in low-income countries are known as DIBs and considered as a way to involve impact investors in the funding of international development projects that focus on the outcomes achieved.

A classic SIB scheme involves a plurality of stakeholders, as shown in Figure 3.6. On the one hand, we have the private sector, encompassing both private impact investors (providing the capital to fund the project) and service providers (bringing unique expertise in innovative service delivery approaches). On the other hand, we have the public sector, which sets the social goals and has the capacity to develop an overarching coordination framework. An independent evaluator usually measures the impact of the project according to predetermined outcome metrics. In terms of financial structure, despite their name, SIBs are not bond-like instruments, but they have been mainly funded through private debt and equity. Given that this model has been generally applied to small-scale projects, at the local level, and with a quite variable return, they have been mainly funded by foundations and impact-first investors (Vecchi & Casalini, 2019).

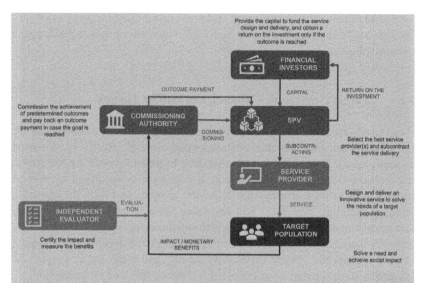

Source: Authors' elaboration, based on Casalini and Vecchi (2021).

Figure 3.6   The social impact bond scheme

An example of an SIB is the Essex Edge of Care project, commissioned by the local authority, Essex County Council, in the UK, and focused on preventing young people aged 11 to 17 with significant behavioral problems from entering care. The SIB provided multisystemic therapy, delivered by Action for Children, a charitable service provider, and it was funded by eight impact investors with a total commitment of GPB 3.1 million. The financial return for these investors was linked to the success of the program in helping children remain out of care and safely at home with their families. As a result of the SIB project, a reduction of over 96,000 days spent in care was achieved amongst the service users, compared to a historical baseline, including savings of GPB 17.9 million.

Several criticisms were raised concerning the low replicability and scalability of the SIB model as a target of II at the global level (see, for example, Arena et al., 2016; Vecchi & Casalini, 2019). In particular, one of the key issues is that, following the model promoted by the UK government, the focus of SIBs has been much more on the realization of savings in the public budget as a result of improved outcomes, rather than on the improved outcomes themselves (e.g., savings in police, courts, prison, probation, etc., due to lower recidivism rates, rather than the value of lower recidivism rates for society). This approach has induced governments, service providers, and impact investors alike to prefer more standard programs and to only focus on those service areas where there is the potential to achieve savings, rather than to scale up this model as a way to innovate welfare service provision and achieve long-term impact.

3.2   Target Geographies, Sectors, and Impact Themes

II can be practiced in both developed and emerging countries, as both areas are facing social and environmental challenges that could be effectively addressed by innovative hybrid social business models. From an investor's perspective, the decision to target a specific region or country may be driven by several reasons, such as their affinity with a specific geographical area, the existence of local expertise, networks, and resources, as well as impact objectives. Investors from developing markets tend to support enterprises addressing challenges in their home countries, while investors from the developed world have varying approaches – some invest only locally, and many target developing markets or have separate allocations for II domestically and internationally.

According to GIIN, almost 60 percent of AuM in the II market worldwide is invested in enterprises in emerging markets – including all regions outside of North America, Western Europe, and Oceania. While II in emerging markets is still dominated by capital provided by Western investors, the situation is changing as the concept of II gains momentum among local wealth holders, who are increasingly incorporating social and environmental objectives into their family businesses, investments, and foundations.

In terms of sectors, II covers a broad range of industries, including the climate and environment, education, employment and workforce development, energy, financial services, food and agriculture, health, housing and community, and water and sanitation. What differentiates II from purely sector-specific investing is that II usually targets an impact theme rather than simply a sector (Balandina Jaquier, 2016). An impact theme can address challenges that span across different sectors (e.g., addressing raising levels of education of low-income population as a strategy for poverty alleviation can result in developing an innovative affordable education technology – education sector; or alternatively providing the solar electrification of off-grid rural villages, which has proven to result in a lower school dropout rate by providing better-quality and cheaper lighting – energy sector).

II in emerging markets usually tackles impact themes related to the access of affordable and better-quality infrastructure and services to low-income communities (i.e., the so-called bottom of the pyramid), therefore, key target sectors include education, energy, financial services, food and agriculture, health, affordable housing, and water and sanitation. II in mature markets tends to address themes such as gaps in public-sector provision of social services, demographic changes, and new emerging social needs, with key target sectors being the climate and environment, employment and workforce development, healthcare, family, and elderly care. Leveraging the IRIS+ Thematic Taxonomy,[12] Table 3.1 provides an overview of the main sectors and impact themes in II, including some selected examples of II solutions that address the impact themes.

4.   MEASURING THE IMPACT IN IMPACT INVESTING

One hallmark of II is the commitment to measure and manage impact, known as impact measurement and management (IMM). IMM is integral to making effective impact investment, as it provides evidence of the social or environmental performance of investees and further legitimizes II as an investment approach intended to achieve additionality.

Ever since II was officially born in 2007, IMM has dominated the debate about this investment approach. Much of the debate, both in academia and practice, has been focused on developing pragmatic, cost-effective, and replicable methodologies and sets of indicators for measuring the effectiveness of intervention in achieving a range of outcomes and impact. However, since what is being measured is rarely quantifiable as a single number, such as a dollar value, or a quantity, and it is unlikely to be standardized across different contexts and investees, there is widespread consensus that there is no one size fits all. Over the past ten years, significant empirical and practical research in this field has been undertaken and supported by coordinated initiatives, such as the Expert Group on Social Business on Impact Measurement created by the European Commission, the Impact Measurement Working Group of the task force on social impact investment set up by the G8, the Operating Principles for Impact Management promoted by the International Finance Corporation, as well as industry associations including, inter alia, GIIN with their IRIS framework, the Impact Management Project, the Global Reporting Initiative (GRI), and the B Lab with their Global Impact Investment Rating System (GIIRS). Thanks to these efforts, a variety of measurement standards, tools, and frameworks have matured alongside the industry, as summarized in Table 3.2.

According to GIIN, while their original Annual Impact Investor Survey, produced ten years ago, revealed that the overwhelming majority of impact investors did not adopt an IMM system or used proprietary systems, a decade later, a significant shift has seen standard IMM systems in widespread adoption across the industry. Most commonly, investors and asset managers use alignment to the SDGs (73 percent of respondents report use for at least one

Table 3.1   *Target sectors, impact themes, and selected examples of solutions*

Sector	Main impact themes	Selected examples of impact investing solutions
Climate and environment	Biodiversity and ecosystem conservation Climate change mitigation Pollution and waste reduction	Control, management, and eradication of invasive species Habitat conservation and restoration services Bioproducts and biochemicals Carbon capture, storage, and sequestration Cradle-to-cradle systems
Education	Access to inclusive and quality education for all Lifelong learning opportunities	Student development (including curricula, facilities, teacher training, teaching materials, and targeted support) Alternative affordable schools, tools, platforms, and training programs (including employment-readiness training and services)
Employment and workforce development	Earnings, wealth, and social integration through employment and entrepreneurship (especially for disadvantaged groups)	Job skills improvement (upskilling, lifelong learning, and technical and vocational training) Job stability improvement (including investment to improve informal or gig jobs, and terms and conditions of employment)
Energy	Energy access Clean energy Energy efficiency	Generation, transmission, distribution, and storage of energy from renewable sources Products, services, and technologies to provide quality energy access at lower cost to underserved groups and communities (including lighting, phone charging, and household appliances, etc.)
Financial services	Financial inclusion for marginalized individuals and industries, and small/micro enterprises	Micro finance Refugee finance Inclusive digital finance (including digital models that enable mobile payments, personal financial management, or advisory, insuretech, and savings platforms)
Food and agriculture	Environmentally and socially sustainable agriculture Food security	Agricultural education and capacity building Agricultural information and communications technology, precision farming Food production, distribution, and consumption (including retail, transport, storage, enrichment, solar drying, and food safety) Supply chain strengthening and market linkage

Sector	Main impact themes	Selected examples of impact investing solutions
Health	Inclusive and quality health services, medicines, vaccines, technologies, and financing to ensure health and well-being for all	Medical, mental, and well-being health services delivered through accessible clinics, laboratories, hospitals, and community health workers, or other means Affordable health supplies (including medicines, vaccines, and equipment) Health education Health insurance and financing
Housing and community	Access to high-quality, affordable housing Sustainable and accessible community facilities	Affordable housing acquisition, development, and preservation Supportive housing services (including employment, physical and mental health services, rental subsidies, and links to public transport)
Water and sanitation	Consistent, reliable, and affordable access to clean, safe, and drinkable water and sanitation	Water conservation (including watershed management and restoration) Water production (including rainwater harvesting) Water treatment (including desalination, wastewater treatment, and water filtration) Sanitation (sewered and non-sewered services, products, and infrastructure)

Source: Adapted from IRIS+.

purpose). One of the advantages related to the use of the SDGs is that they are a universal tool, which makes reporting easier, giving a framework to structure investment and offering a broad overview of the development area. However, the limits of SDGs have been stated to be too high level and a system that could end up being used as a marketing tool (van Raak & Raaphorst, 2020). Other popularly used frameworks are the IRIS Catalog of Metrics (46 percent), IRIS+ Core Metrics Sets (36 percent), and the Impact Management Project's five dimensions of impact convention (32 percent).[13] It must be noted that most investors tend to use a blend of these frameworks and IMM systems, and not just a single one, to help them understand, measure, and report their impact.

Even if these frameworks and tools have helped build consensus on how to shape IMM and classify, measure, and report impact, a vast amount of urgent work is still needed to produce evidence around the kinds of investment that create the highest additionality.

5.　THE WAY FORWARD

Just over ten years ago, the II market was projected to reach between USD 400 billion and USD 1 trillion in AuM by 2020[14] in a forecast that, at the time,

Table 3.2   Commonly applied impact management and measurement framework

Impact management and measurement framework	Scope of the framework	Key features
Alignment with the SDGs	Defining impact targets and shaping impact management and measurement processes	Impact investors usually target impact themes aligned to one or more of the SDGs. In addition to target setting, impact investors often use the SDGs to guide their impact measurement practice by mapping investments to the SDGs and channeling capital towards SDG-aligned priorities.
International Finance Corporation Operating Principles for Impact Management	Shaping impact management and measurement processes	The nine Impact Principles are a framework for the design and implementation of impact management systems, ensuring that impact considerations are integrated throughout the investment lifecycle. They do not prescribe specific measurement tools and indicators.
The Impact Management Project	Defining dimensions of impact	The Impact Management Project identifies five key dimensions that help investors and investees understand their social and environmental impact in a common way: who, what, how much, risk, and contribution.
GIIN IRIS Catalog of Metrics	Measuring and reporting impact results	IRIS is a catalogue of more than 600 standardized performance metrics (indicators), divided by focus (e.g., social versus environmental), sector, and impact theme.
GIIN IRIS+ Core Metrics Sets	Measuring and reporting impact results	In 2019, the IRIS Catalog was expanded by including shortlists of key impact performance indicators – built on standard IRIS metrics and backed by evidence and best practice – aligned to common impact themes and the SDGs.
Global Reporting Initiative (GRI)	Measuring and reporting impact results	The Global Reporting Initiative Standards allow an organization to report information in a way that covers all of its most significant impact on the economy, environment, and people, or to focus only on specific topics, such as climate change or child labor. There are universal standards, sector standards, and topic standards.
B Lab Global Impact Investment Rating System (GIIRS)	Measuring and reporting impact results	The Global Impact Investment Rating System is a catalogue of over 300 indicators that companies can adopt to see how they stack up against top performers like Certified B Corporations.

seemed very ambitious to many of those who read it. At the beginning, the II community was populated by a few pioneer actors with a strong commitment to identify and implement innovative business models to solve pressing societal challenges. In a nutshell, these actors were entrepreneurs with a core social mission alongside the profit motive aiming at contributing with new solutions to the needs of communities; intermediaries, such as asset management firms, providing capital as well as hands-on support to them; and ultimate investors – asset owners – choosing to allocate part of their resources to these investees, even accepting lower financial returns or longer payback periods.

A decade later, the market has grown even more steadily than projected, with unprecedented capital flowing into this space and many of the world's largest investment firms creating dedicated funds and products. In an era when "sustainability" is a catchword, the concept of II has become increasingly attractive, thanks to its promises to deliver both impact and returns. Many mainstream investors, who, in the early days were skeptical and found it difficult to categorize II within their traditional asset allocation, are now eager to commit more capital to the II space. While they are bringing scale to the industry, the crucial issue is whether beyond these capital flows there is real additionality, namely the intentional search for innovative solutions that can generate more impact than existing models.

With the rapid growth of the market, II seems to lose its fundamental characteristics and simply becomes a refocusing of traditional investing, by targeting profitable companies that have a purpose in some way related to the SDGs, rather than innovative impact solutions that, thanks to a redesign of the value chain, can provide an answer to societal challenges with a viable business model. This phenomenon is quite evident in venture capital, where, according to the latest report about the state of European tech by Atomico and Orrick,[15] a number of traditional venture capital firms are marketing themselves as having impact and more than 20 percent of investments in Europe are directed towards what they call "purpose-driven tech companies."

The risk of "impact washing" is high, as II becomes more an advertising gimmick than a real force to drive change, where II funds that promise both impact and higher yields, at least in the short term, are able to raise more capital. In this scenario, even asset managers strongly anchored to the original idea of II risk losing their DNA and therefore being moved towards more profitable investment approaches that have little to do with the concept of additionality. What is happening, albeit on a different scale, is not very far from what happened in ESG investing, which has recently taken center stage due to a debate on the lack of credibility of commitments made by companies.

To grow II over the next ten years, greater improvements in measurements and standards to soothe raising concerns about the integrity of the field are needed. The regulatory efforts under way to better regulate ESG investments and the pressure to measure the so-called impact-weighted profit coming from various think tanks, such as the one led by Sir Ronald Cohen, one of the founding fathers of II, will help to create a clearer diversification between what generates additionality and what is simply socially compliant or profit with purpose.

NOTES

1. GIIN (2020), Annual Impact Investor Survey. Available at: https://thegiin.org/research/publication/impinv-survey-2020, accessed March 11, 2022.
2. Global Sustainable investment Alliance (2021), Global Sustainable Investment Review. Available at: www.gsi-alliance.org/wp-content/uploads/2021/08/GSIR-20201.pdf, accessed March 11, 2022.
3. International Finance Corporation (2021), Investing for Impact: The Global Impact Investing Market 2020. Available at: www.ifc.org/wps/wcm/connect/publications_ext_content/ifc_external_publication_site/publications_listing_page/impact-investing-market-2020, accessed March 11, 2022.
4. World Economic Forum (2021), Charting the Course for SDG Financing in the Decade of Delivery. Available at: www.weforum.org/agenda/2020/01/unlocking-sdg-financing-decade-delivery/, accessed March 11, 2022.
5. European Commission (2020), European Commission Report on the Impact of Demographic Change. Available at: https://ec.europa.eu/info/sites/default/files/demography_report_2020_n.pdf, accessed March 11, 2022.
6. Global Entrepreneurship Monitor (2016), Report on Social Entrepreneurship. Available at: www.gemconsortium.org/report/gem-2015-report-on-social-entrepreneurship, accessed March 11, 2022.
7. Capgemini (2021), World Wealth Report. Available at: https://worldwealthreport.com, accessed March 11, 2022.
8. GIIN (2018), A Resource for Structuring Blended Finance Vehicles. Available at: https://thegiin.org/assets/upload/Blended%20Finance%20Resource%20-%20GIIN.pdf, accessed March 11, 2022.
9. Cambridge Associate & GIIN (2015), Introducing the Impact Investing Benchmark. Available at: https://thegiin.org/assets/documents/pub/Introducing_the_Impact_Investing_Benchmark.pdf, accessed March 11, 2022.
10. JPMorgan (2010), Impact Investments: An Emerging Asset Class. Available at: https://thegiin.org/assets/documents/Impact%20Investments%20an%20Emerging%20Asset%20Class2.pdf, accessed March 11, 2022.
11. World Economic Forum (2013), From the Margins to the Mainstream: Assessment of the Impact Investment Sector and Opportunities to Engage Mainstream Investors. Available at: www3.weforum.org/docs/WEF_II_FromMarginsMainstream_Report_2013.pdf, accessed March 11, 2022.
12. GIIN (2019), IRIS+ Thematic Taxonomy. Available at: https://iris.thegiin.org/document/iris-thematic-taxonomy/, accessed March 11, 2022.
13. As reported by GIIN in the Annual Impact Investor Survey.
14. See JPMorgan (2010), Impact Investments: An Emerging Asset Class, p. 39.
15. Atomico & Orrick (2021), The State of European Tech 2020. Available at: https://2020.stateofeuropeantech.com/, accessed March 11, 2022.

4.   Unlocking private capital through blended finance

1.   BLENDED FINANCE: A BROADER DEFINITION

"Blending" is a common term in development finance that means, with a broader meaning, mixing public and private financial resources to sustain social and economic development.

In recent years, development finance has increasingly emerged as a tool to reduce inequalities and sustain development in low- and middle-income countries. In this context, blended finance (BF) has been defined, with a narrower perspective, as "the strategic use of public capital and philanthropic funds to mobilize private investment flows towards the achievement of Sustainable Development Goals in emerging and frontier markets" (OECD, 2018).

In this chapter, we adopt a broader perspective to development finance and blending, by not just focusing on developing countries. We conceive BF as a structuring approach, meant to combine together layers of money coming from different investors, with different profiles, mandates, and expectations. Such a blending approach is based on mixing public and private capital in a common and complementary investment scheme where public and/or philanthropic sources are used as a catalyst to increase private-sector investments in markets that are affected by some failures or inefficiencies.

Markets affected by failures or inefficiencies, where BF plays a role, usually show the following characteristics (World Economic Forum, 2015):

- Early stage of development: underdeveloped markets lack the infrastructure, expertise, pools of capital, and connection of supply to demand required to function efficiently; they are usually less liquid, introducing uncertainty about whether an investor will be able to exit the investment and receive their money back.
- Returns are too low for the level of real or perceived risk: return expectations may be hampered by several factors, such as high transaction costs associated with learning new markets and for small-scale deals, lengthy transaction times, etc.

- Knowledge and capability gaps of private investors: private capital providers lack in-depth understanding and competencies, or the level of information asymmetries is too high to accurately assess risk and make informed investment decisions.

These market failures and inefficiencies mostly apply to developing countries; however, they are not limited to these regions. They may also occur in developed economies, in specific areas such as small and medium enterprises' (SMEs) access to credit and innovative start-up access to venture capital (VC), as we will discuss in Section 4.

2.   BLENDED FINANCE CHARACTERISTICS

BF is a form of PPP for development that involves the following actors:

- public investors, those with a development mandate, and those with both a commercial and development mandate, such as various multilateral development banks;
- philanthropic investors, such as foundations; and
- private investors.

A BF approach is based on three principles:

1. Leverage: development finance (including both public and philanthropic funds) is used to attract more private capital through de-risking mechanisms.
2. Impact: BF catalyzes additional resources to fund investments able to drive social, environmental, and economic progress. BF mechanisms allow not only for the mixing of public and private money, but also for the mixing of skills to increase the effectiveness of development-related investments.
3. Returns: investments have different returns, ranging from below market (also called concessionary) to risk-adjusted market rate, depending on the type of investor involved; the goal of BF mechanisms is to generate returns for private investors in line with the market and investor expectations, based on the level of perceived risk.

The concept of additionality is a crucial element in BF. The literature distinguishes between financial additionality (FA) and economic additionality (EA, sometimes referred to as development additionality). FA comes from the additional capital mobilized in the market by private investors, or other positive effects such as a reduction in the cost of funding, following the injection of development funding. EA is the improvement in the overall economy and society due to the increased access to and availability of capital, and it can be ultimately measured in terms of GDP and employment growth, plus more taxes for the government. FA is the output of BF, whereas EA represents its outcome; therefore, while the assessment of FA is important to demonstrate the success of a BF program, it is the assessment of the EA that ultimately matters for the policymaker.

Since the aim of BF is to generate additionality, BF mechanisms should be intended to support quasi-bankable projects, i.e., those investments that are potentially interesting for funders but the level of real or perceived risk is too high. For quasi-bankable projects, BF allows risk mitigation to attract private capital. BF can also support bankable projects, with the aim to act as an anchor investor and increase available funding, or to provide technical assistance for maximizing the impact of the investment. Unbankable projects, and projects that are conceived under a traditional charity approach, are not the focus of BF (Convergence, 2020).

In any case, BF should avoid crowding out private financing and market distortion. Crowding out occurs when public and philanthropic funders invest in a project that would have been viable without any development support. Where this occurs, it not only means that scarce public and philanthropic funding has been misspent, but it also has the potential to distort markets and undermine the development of a healthy private-sector market, reducing the overall funding available for targeted areas in the long term.

3.   BLENDED FINANCE INSTRUMENTS

As discussed previously, BF deliberately uses and mixes financial instruments to catalyze private capital. The three pillars of BF – leverage, impact, and returns – influence how public and philanthropic capital providers structure financial instruments.

First, blending money can happen at diverse levels, at the project or fund level, providing capital directly to recipients or through intermediaries, as shown in Figure 4.1. In most cases, the preferred option is to blend financing at the fund level to generate a higher leverage effect in terms of increased attraction of private capital per single public or philanthropic money invested. Funds are pools of private or public-private capital, where blending occurs at the capital structure level for public-private funds, or at the project level (Convergence, 2020). Development resources come in most cases from facilities, which are earmarked allocations of money. There is no blending of money in these facilities; instead, facilities provide finance to blend further down at the fund or project level.

Second, these resources can be invested through a range of instruments, which include debt, equity, guarantees, grants, and grant-funded technical

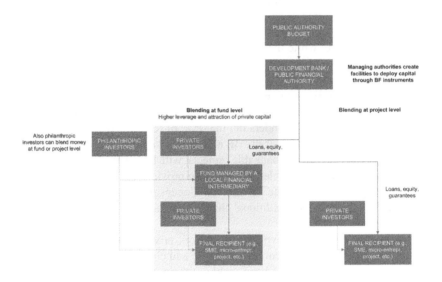

Figure 4.1   Blending mechanisms at the fund or project level

assistance, as shown in Figure 4.2. These BF instruments are used for the following:

- Co-investment of development capital and private capital, both in the form of debt and equity: public or philanthropic investors provide concessional money within a capital structure to lower the overall cost of capital, thus making the project viable, or to provide an additional layer of protection to private investors, thus attracting them. Concessional capital includes first-loss debt or equity, and debt or equity that bears risk at below-market financial returns, to mobilize private-sector investment. The use of concessional capital allows for the financing to be structured with different layers of risk, through:
    - A-shares and senior notes to attract institutional investors;
    - B-shares, such as mezzanine capital provided by private investors with an appetite for risk, or by public investors with a commercial mandate; and
    - junior tranches of debt and first-loss equity shares dedicated to development finance investors (multilateral development banks, donors, or impact investors) with a development mandate. Public investors can also provide co-investments on a "pari passu" basis, i.e., on the same terms and conditions of private funders, acting as anchor investors to demonstrate viability and provide investor comfort.

- Guarantees: public or philanthropic investors provide credit enhancement, or investor protection against capital losses, through guarantees on below-market terms.
- Grants: public or philanthropic investors provide a financial award with no expected repayment or compensation to cover capital, operating expenditures, or financial costs. Grants are inefficient, because they do not stimulate co-investment and additionality of resources; therefore, they should be used to address serious market failures.
- Technical assistance: public or philanthropic investors provide grant-funded technical assistance that can be used before or after the completion of the investment, to strengthen viability and impact. Technical assistance is also helpful to reduce information asymmetries and lower the high transaction and screening costs for investors.

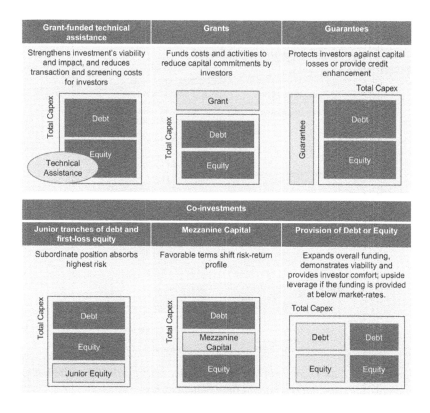

Figure 4.2   Blended finance instruments

In Figures 4.3 and 4.4 there are two examples of BF. The former shows a typical BF fund with different layers of money (as with the JAWEF fund, described in Section 4.3); the latter shows the BF mechanism effect at the beneficiary level thanks to a co-investment of debt at and below the market level.

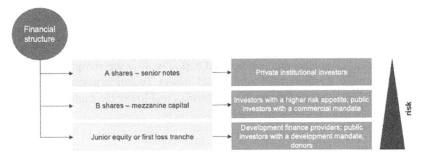

Figure 4.3   *An example of a blended finance instrument: the blending mechanism at the fund level*

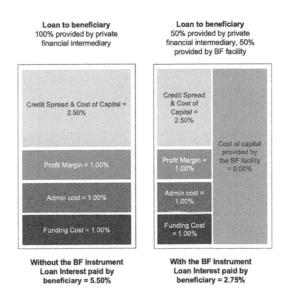

Figure 4.4   *An example of a blended finance instrument: the reduction of the interest rate to final beneficiaries*

4. CASES AND APPLICATIONS OF BLENDED FINANCE INSTRUMENTS

4.1 Credit Guarantee Schemes to Support Small and Medium-Sized Enterprises' Access to Credit

The development of SMEs is a priority for policymakers in many countries across the world, where they have become the focus of governmental economic policies but also one of the main endeavors of regional development banks. The centrality of SMEs depends on their crucial role in improving social cohesion, reducing poverty, and fostering regional and local development. However, their capacity to contribute to economic and social development can be hampered by difficulties in securing finance, such as access to credit (Stiglitz & Weiss, 1981; Cressy, 2002; Abraham & Schmukler, 2017). In fact, it is widely recognized that SMEs have limited external funding capacity compared to larger firms, although they are more dependent on bank loans and are more exposed to financial turmoil. There are four main reasons why they have difficulties when trying to access bank finance: information asymmetry, high administrative costs for small-scale lending, high-risk perception, and lack of collateral.

Credit guarantee schemes (CGS) are one of the dominant approaches to support SMEs' access to credit, with more than 2,250 CGS worldwide (among others, Italy has the largest guarantee system in place in Europe; see Box 4.1 about the Italian Central Guarantee Fund).

BOX 4.1 THE ITALIAN CENTRAL GUARANTEE FUND

Fondo Centrale di Garanzia (FCG) is the main Italian public CGS designed to improve access to credit and thus support the economic growth of micro, small, and medium-sized enterprises. Though FCG has been active since 2000, its role in the framework of Italian SME financial enhancement policies was strengthened during the great financial crisis, and further increased during the Covid-19 pandemic; it was refinanced with approximately EUR 2 billion between 2008 and 2012, then by EUR 1.2 billion between 2013 and 2014, and finally by an additional EUR 7.5 billion in 2020.

The Italian guarantee system is one of the largest in Europe and it shows a multilayer structure. For this reason, the lending and guarantee process involves different players: the applicant SME, FCG, as well as other financial intermediaries, which are banks or mutual guarantee institutions (MGIs). Three guarantees can be provided by FCG: counter-guarantees and co-guarantees are given to MGIs acting, in the first case, as first-level guarantors or, in the second case, as co-guarantor along with MGIs; direct guarantees can also be provided to banks, which can apply directly for FCG guarantee at the central national level, bypassing the system of local and regional MGIs.

Typically, the guarantee issued by FCG does not cover the entire amount of the loan; the coverage rate can reach 80 percent of the loan in the case of direct guarantees, and 90 percent for a counter-guarantee to an MGI. The maximum amount of loan that can be guaranteed is EUR 5 million. FCG applies a fee to guaranteed companies, which is approximately within a range from 0.25 percent up to 3 percent of the guaranteed amount, depending on the type of operation and guarantee.

To sustain the Italian SMEs during the period hit the hardest by the pandemic, the Italian government extended the possibility for FCG's guarantee to cover up to 100 percent (only for small loans under EUR 25,000) and reduced the fee for guaranteed companies down to zero. In 2020, FCG experienced an incredible increase in applications, and issued guarantees for EUR 105.9 billion, allowing more than 1.5 million SMEs to get access to EUR 124.4 billion in lending overall,[1] with a leverage effect of 1:16, as shown in Figure 4.5.

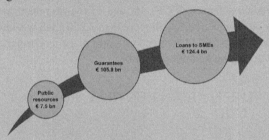

Source: Authors, based on the figures publicly available at www.fondidigaranzia.it/numeri-del-fondo/, accessed March 22, 2022.

Figure 4.5   The leverage effect of the Italian FCG

Empirical studies (e.g., Ferrando & Rossolini, 2015; Caselli et al., 2019) confirmed that FCG generated both FA and EA on the guarantees issued during the period of economic downturn of the great financial crisis. More time is needed to observe the results of the guarantees issued during the Covid-19 pandemic.

CGS are programs, usually funded by public money, aimed at reducing financial banking losses in cases of borrower default. From a public-sector perspective, the biggest advantage of CGS as BF instruments is high financial leverage, which allows public funders to guarantee loans multiple times bigger than CGS capital funds. From an SME perspective, CGS are considered one possible solution to the aforementioned problems that companies face when accessing the financial system – they can reduce information asymmetry, thanks to the scoring models used and assessment of firm eligibility. In addition, when credit is guaranteed, the lender faces lower risk and, therefore, can offer better lending conditions and require lower collateral.

Since the aim of CGS is to generate additional benefit, the provision of a guarantee should not be solely aimed at companies which, in any case, can access the banking system. For this reason, the additionality of CGS can be measured in terms of FA (i.e., benefits such as the increase in resources allocated by the banking system, including the increase in the size of loans or extension in loan maturities, reduction of the interest rates applied to loans, reduction of transaction costs, and reduced amount of collateral), and EA (i.e., improvement in the overall economy due to the increased access to and availability of capital for SMEs). While there is widespread agreement regarding the FA of public guarantees, evidence in terms of EA is more limited. A number of studies demonstrate a positive impact of CGS on the employment growth rate (e.g., Bradshaw, 2002; Riding et al., 2007; Lelarge et al., 2010), while the positive effect of the guarantee on sales and profit growth is not confirmed in all countries.

4.2   Public-Private Venture Capital to Sustain the Creation of Innovative Start-Ups

VC is a form of financial intermediation particularly well suited to support the creation and growth of innovative enterprises at an early stage of development (i.e., start-ups). VC is a means not only to provide equity, but also hands-on support through market expertise, managerial and entrepreneurial skills, and a network of contacts to help start-ups exploit their growth potential.

For these reasons, VC is widely recognized to be a catalyst for entrepreneurship, facilitating the emergence of high-growth firms and innovation and the capitalization and commercialization of R&D activities (Florida & Kenney, 1988; Hood, 2000; Kortum & Lerner, 2000; Lerner & Watson, 2008). In addition, VC has proven to be good for stimulating the creation of skilled managers and entrepreneurship (Popov & Roosenboom, 2009). In other words, VC acts like a form of proximity capital, a factor of institutional thickness, since it provides access to finance, expertise, and a network of relations, thus enhancing the building of social capital at the regional level (Mason, 2009).

However, since the risk embedded in funding innovative ventures at an early stage of development is high, as well as the appraisal and monitoring costs, which are fixed regardless of the size of the deal, the VC market is underdeveloped and start-ups experience an equity gap.

Given the importance of VC, public intervention in the market has been a pillar of both innovation policies and entrepreneurship policies worldwide, with many supranational, national, and state/regional governments that established schemes in support of the VC market. Government schemes are intended to support both demand and supply of VC funding; on the one hand, they strive to improve business innovation, growth, and investment readiness (i.e., demand-side intervention), while, on the other hand, they aim to close the funding gap (i.e., supply-side intervention), particularly for small high-technology firms or in particular regions.

Direct supply-side government schemes, intended to leverage public money to attract private investors in the market, are widely used, with 19 percent of start-ups having received funding from government-supported VC funds globally[2] (see Boxes 4.2 and 4.3 to review the two largest public programs available worldwide, established in the US and in Europe). Even if such direct supply-side government schemes can take many different configurations at the international level, they inject money into the VC market either at the project or fund level. Based on a review of the programs available worldwide, we can distinguish between three types of programs, as follows:

1. Direct public, or public-private, VC investment funds: public money is invested directly, either alone or together with other private limited partners, into selected start-ups. The public competent authority has an active role in the governance of the fund and in the selection and monitoring process of portfolio companies.
2. Public funds of funds: public money is not invested directly into start-ups, but into fully private and already operating VC funds, always together with other private limited partners. Investment decisions are entirely delegated to the private asset management company that operates the VC fund, even if the public competent authority usually has a role in the definition of the investment strategy.
3. Government loans to VC funds: public money is invested into fully private and already operating VC funds, but in the form of a loan; in this case, the public competent authority is not a limited partner in the VC fund and it has a less active role, as it does not contribute to the definition of the investment strategy.

Moving from the first to the last type of direct supply-side government schemes, the level of public financial commitment decreases as it increases the leveraging effects that can be generated by the type of financial instrument. In addition, public money can be provided pari passu, or with some forms of incentive, such as downside protections (through which the competent public authority assumes a share of losses of the private investors) and upside leverages (aimed at providing the private investors with the opportunity to uplift their returns).

BOX 4.2 THE SMALL BUSINESS INVESTMENT COMPANY PROGRAM IN THE UNITED STATES

The Small Business Investment Company (SBIC) program was created by the Small Business Administration (SBA) in 1958. Its primary objective is to facilitate the flow of capital to small businesses to stimulate the national economy. From the inception of the SBIC program to December 31, 2020, SBICs have invested approximately USD 103.5 billion in approximately 184,135 financings to small businesses.[3] The SBA does not make direct investments in small businesses. Instead, privately owned and managed SBA-licensed SBICs provide small businesses with private capital that the SBIC has raised (called regulatory capital) and funds that the SBIC borrows at favorable rates because the SBA guarantees the debenture (loan obligation). This mechanism provides an upside leverage to private investors, as their returns are leveraged thanks to the favorable interest rate applicable on the SBA loan (the interest rate was at 1.034 percent in 2020, nearly half of the previously lowest price of 2.051 percent in 2019).

One of the primary criteria for licensure as a SBIC and being entitled to receive a loan from the SBA is having qualified management. For instance, at least two principals (general partners or equivalent) with substantive and analogous principal investment experience and evidence of a strong rate of business proposals and investment offers (deal flow) in the investment area proposed for the new fund are among the SBIC eligibility requirements. On the side of the firm, only funds that invest in businesses that meet the SBA's definition of "small" may participate in the SBIC program, and 51 percent of employees and assets must be within the US.

Since 2009, the SBIC program has increased its focus on minorities by increasing the amount of leverage available to SBICs that invest at least 50 percent in underserved small businesses (defined as a business owned by women, veterans, or minorities, or located in underserved geographic areas, which includes low- and moderate-income areas). In more recent years, in 2011, the SBA launched the Impact Investment Fund with a USD 1 billion pilot initiative to capitalize investment funds that seek both financial and social return.

BOX 4.3   THE EUROPEAN INVESTMENT FUND'S EQUITY INITIATIVES IN EUROPE

The EIF is the leading player in the European VC market, providing more than EUR 15 billion to more than 750 European VC funds between 2014 and 2019.[4] The EIF's equity signature deals in support of the VC market fall under the umbrella of either the InnovFin or COSME initiatives, which are the key long-lasting and pan-European equity programs offered by the EIF.

The EIF adopts an intermediated model in the form of fund of funds, which entails acting as a limited partner in privately managed VC funds, in charge of making the investment. The EIF provides funding to private VC funds in the form of equity, at the same rate, acting as anchor investor and providing no more than 49 percent of the total funding (at least 51 percent must be provided by independent private investors).

EIF investments in VC funds follow a detailed due diligence process, focusing on various aspects of the investment proposal. In order to be selected, several requirements have to be satisfied. The conditions entail the management team (e.g., experience and composition of the team), the market (e.g., identification, size, growth potential), the deal flow (e.g., track record of access to deals, quality of deals, credibility of plans), the investment strategy (e.g., coherence with the purpose of the EIF, identification of exit routes), the size of the fund, the proposed terms (e.g., legal and tax structure), the expected returns (e.g., financial viability), and the investor base (e.g., support from other investors, co-investment strategy, and rationale). Beyond the initial due diligence, the EIF assesses and monitors its portfolio funds during the whole investment cycle. The EIF is represented in advisory boards or similar investor representation bodies, and VC funds provide the EIF with quarterly and annual reporting. Furthermore, in full compliance with the independence of the management company operating the VC fund, it takes an active role in the case that either the fund's investment team or the investment strategy significantly changes.

In 2012, the EIF set up the SIA facility to support the creation of the II market in Europe. Also SIA operates as a fund of funds managed by the EIF, and it invests in social impact funds which strategically target "fully self-sustainable" and "commercially viable" social enterprises across Europe. SIA reached its final closing in 2015 at the size of EUR 243 million, combining resources from the EIB Group and external investors, including Credit Cooperatif, Deutsche Bank, as well as the Finnish group SITRA and the Bulgarian Development Bank.

4.3 Developing Micro-Finance Programs for the Empowerment of Women in Developing Countries

As discussed above, SME access to credit is important for enhancing social and economic development. This is particularly true in developing countries, where people living at the bottom of the pyramid face significant barriers in accessing finance, which hampers their empowerment and participation across all sectors of the economy.

International BF facilities have emerged to provide financing – and often technical assistance – to micro-finance institutions (MFIs) as a response to address the failure of the traditional financial system to serve these clients, which are usually considered unbankable due to high information asymmetries and risk perceptions. Despite the number of micro-finance initiatives world-wide, access to finance by female entrepreneurs still remains a daunting task. Most MFIs, in fact, provide a lower percentage of micro loans to women, or on average women's loan sizes are smaller (United Nations Development Fund for Women, 2015).

Given the pivotal role of women in society in building stronger economies, and improving quality of life for families and communities, a number of initiatives are now targeting women, with the aim to close the gender gap and advance female empowerment through the provision of financing, products, and services to women and girls (see Box 4.4 about the Japan ASEAN Women Empowerment Fund).

BOX 4.4 THE JAPAN ASEAN WOMEN EMPOWERMENT FUND

In 2016, the impact investment manager BlueOrchard established the Japan ASEAN Women Empowerment Fund (JAWEF)[5] to address the significant financing gap faced by women in the Association of Southeast Asian Nations (ASEAN) region and beyond.

The fund provides debt financing to MFIs for on-lending to female entrepreneurs across different ASEAN countries, including Cambodia, Myanmar, Philippines, Vietnam, Laos, Malaysia, and Indonesia, as well as India, Pakistan, and Sri Lanka. The MFIs must either disproportionately target female borrowers (at least 60 percent) that have or intend to develop specific products for female empowerment. Eligible products include credit and leasing, savings, insurance, payments and remittances, pensions services, or mobile banking for the purposes of income generation, housing, education (including the education of family members), health, water and sanitation, or energy efficiency.

JAWEF achieved first close in 2016, with a size of USD 120.5 million, and a final close of USD 241 million in 2019. Specifically, JAWEF appealed to institutional investors looking to enter new sectors (i.e., micro finance) and new geographies (i.e., developing markets). Given the limited exposure of institutional investors to these markets, the tiered structure of the fund – including the presence of both first-loss and mezzanine capital – provided the necessary risk mitigation to support their appetite to invest.

In particular, as shown in Figure 4.6, JAWEF is a three-tiered blended finance fund, consisting of the following classes of shares:

- Junior shares: these act as a first loss for JAWEF, ranked as subordinate to the mezzanine and senior tranches. Junior shares are held by BlueOrchard and Summit Financial and represent just 0.5 percent of the aggregate value of the fund. This tranche is intended to cover losses due to deterioration in credit quality and currency risks related to portfolio investments. To date, these funds have not been used thanks to the solid fund performance.
- Mezzanine shares: these are two concessional mezzanine tranches, individually negotiated with Japan Bank for International Cooperation and Japan International Cooperation Agency. These tranches rank junior in repayment and receive lower returns than the senior tranche.
- Senior shares: these shares rank as the most senior in the capital structure and target institutional investors, including Sumitomo Life Insurance Company and the Sasakawa Peace Foundation.

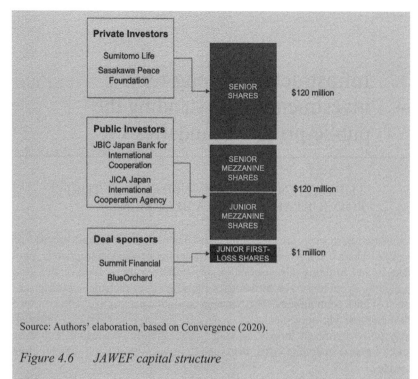

Source: Authors' elaboration, based on Convergence (2020).

Figure 4.6   JAWEF capital structure

To date, JAWEF has provided 38 loans to 24 MFIs, reaching 250,000 beneficiary micro entrepreneurs, of which 91 percent of end borrowers are wom-
en and 78 percent are rural clients.

NOTES

1. www.fondidigaranzia.it/numeri-del-fondo/, accessed March 11, 2022.
2. In Europe, this percentage is even higher, with 30 percent of firms that have
    received funding from government-supported VC funds (Thomson One Banker).
3. www.sba.gov/partners/sbics, accessed March 11, 2022.
4. www.eif.org/news_centre/publications/eif-annual-report-2019.htm, accessed March
    11, 2022.
5. The case described in the box is based onConvergence, Japan ASEAN Women
    Empowerment Fund Case Study. Available at: www.convergence.finance/resource/
    5AR5njuJR45khZMkblhjOa/view, accessed March 11, 2022.

5. Infrastructure as long-term investment: understanding the public-private boundaries

1. THE SALIENT ROLE OF INFRASTRUCTURE FOR SUSTAINABLE DEVELOPMENT

Infrastructure systems are crucial for a sustainable socio-economic progress of nations. Their development, when projects are not handled appropriately, may take its toll in terms of consumption of natural resources, biodiversity loss, pollution, greenhouse gas emissions, cultural heritage damage, and displacement of local communities. Also, from an economic perspective, infrastructure development and implementation, especially for large and complex projects, may pose significant threats, leaving public authorities sagging with debt and long-term operating costs, bankrupting private developers, with no clear upside.

The global need for substantial infrastructure and contribution to sustainable development was widely recognized well before Covid-19. However, in the wake of the pandemic, quality and more resilient infrastructure has come under greater focus as societies face strained health systems, disruption in supply chains, increasing unemployment, deflationary pressures in energy markets, and disruption in transportation.[1] According to the Global Infrastructure Hub – a G20 initiative – the infrastructure gap globally amounts to USD 15 trillion, and USD 18 trillion if we also consider the investments needed to achieve the SDGs. It should be noted that this value only refers to economic infrastructure,[2] therefore not representing the infrastructural gap for social sectors, such as health, education, and affordable/social housing. In Europe, SDA Bocconi estimated an infrastructure gap in health and education of about EUR 1 trillion (Cusumano et al., 2017).[3] At the global level, the total annual infrastructure gap is estimated at USD 6.3 trillion per year until 2030 to support growth and equal development, and to close it the annual infrastructure investment would need to increase from 3.0 to 3.5 percent of global gross domestic product (OECD, 2017).

In the short term, increased expenditure on infrastructure will have an immediate effect on global post-pandemic recovery, by boosting employment, supporting economic growth, and spending on construction activities. In a recent analysis, the Global Infrastructure Hub showed that the short-term fiscal multiplier of infrastructure investments, on average, reached 0.80 within one year, and 1.53 within two to five years (Global Infrastructure Hub, 2020). In the medium to long term, infrastructure plays an increasingly pivotal role for the achievement of the SDGs and in the relaunch of economies through spending on renewable energies and decarbonization policies.

Mobilizing LTIs is key to supplying the resources needed to sustain such an effort not only from a financial perspective, especially given the fiscal outlook resulting from Covid-19, but also because it may help to integrate sustainability, thanks to the long-term perspective, delving deeper into how infrastructure projects are selected, planned, designed, financed, and delivered. To this end, in 2019, the G20, recognizing that "the world still faces a massive gap in financing for investment in new and existing infrastructure, which could generate a serious bottleneck to economic growth and development or provision of secure and reliable public services" in order to mobilize private capital and "develop infrastructure as an asset class, and maximising the positive impact of infrastructure investment," endorsed a set of principles for promoting not only quantity, but also quality of infrastructure investment. Such principles are:

- maximizing the positive impact of infrastructure to achieve sustainable growth and development;
- raising economic efficiency in view of lifecycle costs;
- integrating environmental considerations in infrastructure investments;
- building resilience against natural disasters and other risks;
- integrating social considerations in infrastructure investments; and
- strengthening infrastructure governance.

2.   INTEGRATING A LONG-TERM QUALITY PERSPECTIVE IN THE INFRASTRUCTURE LIFECYCLE

Before discussing how LTIs can be involved in infrastructure development and financing, it may be useful to acknowledge the infrastructure lifecycle. Starting from the very beginning, policies set the framework – in terms of objectives, rules, and resources – within which strategies and infrastructure projects are designed. Infrastructure planning translates policy priorities into programs/ projects by identifying specific needs to be addressed, setting priorities and defining the strategy which is most suitable to deliver a project efficiently, and effectively, among other things, the degree of involvement of the private sector in reaching policy goals. The strategy definition encompasses at least three levels of decision, as suggested by Estache et al. (2009):

1. Governments must decide whether to develop infrastructure and deliver the related services in-house or procure them from the market.
2. If governments decide to procure goods and services from the market, the next decision is how to align authorities and responsibilities with stakeholders. There are different stakeholders that can conduct some parts of the process, including ownership. Relevant questions at this step are:
    a. Who should own infrastructure?
    b. Who should operate it?
    c. Who should invest in public assets?
    d. Under what circumstances could those tasks be delegated to different agents?
    e. What circumstances call for bundling them together under a single agent?

    While bundling everything under state ownership means nationalization of infrastructure, unbundling some of the tasks can represent some forms of private-sector participation in infrastructure, which we identify with the broad use of the term PPP.
3. If the whole of the process is delegated to market players, it is fundamental to decide how to design a selection process able to foster competition, lower information asymmetries (which can lead to an adverse selection), and reward the good behavior of contractors (thus lowering the risk of moral hazard).

The first and second decisions pave the way to the different delivery models that are presented and discussed in the next section. It is worth noting that a generalization of such delivery models is difficult because many nuances exist across jurisdictions.

Regarding the third decision, there is a growing consensus that procurement – both in the public and private sectors – should be used as a strategic lever for systematically and transparently promoting an organization's social, environmental, and economic goals across its entire supply chain. Proponents of this approach also argue that, by incorporating a broader set of measures into procurement, an organization may improve its long-term performance and accountability towards its relevant stakeholders. This is of paramount importance for the public sector but, as argued in Chapter 2, also for corporations as they are trying to integrate stakeholder perspectives into their business practices. The task is challenging for at least two reasons. First, adopting a quality approach – which in practical terms may entail mandating the adoption of best available technologies and circular economy solutions, requiring sustainably sourced materials, asking for environmental certification, improved accessibility for old people or those with disabilities, including a gender perspective of design – increases short-term development costs versus long-term benefits. Second, including ambitious technical specifications may restrict competition to just a few sophisticated suppliers able to meet the tender criteria. To overcome these apparent trade-offs between quality/innovation and upfront costs/ competition the tendering organization shall, as stressed also in the G20 principles for quality investment, carefully assess all design, technical, and delivery options against their lifecycle costs, risks, and potential benefits.

If it is true that such high-quality standards for infrastructure development may reduce competition, it is also true that public authorities should embody a sophisticated buyer approach, in order to achieve wider policy goals through procurement, which are not only those related to environmental and societal impact but also an increased sophistication of economic players' business models.

3.   INFRASTRUCTURE DELIVERY MODELS: WHERE DOES THE MARKET STAND?

Infrastructure can be built and operated through different governance structures: public entities and firms, hybrid models, and markets (Da Cruz & Marques, 2012).

The in-house model consists of the direct involvement of the (local- or state-level) government or other public-sector entities. When there is the need for greater efficiency with a more entrepreneurial and flexible approach to deliver infrastructure, without the hurdles of privatization, the state-owned enterprise (SoE) model can be a reasonable choice. Corporatization in the public sector (Bilodeau et al., 2007) finds its rationale in the hybrid model, based on a public governance structure that incorporates certain features of private enterprises, e.g., clear and stable objectives, incentives for efficiency, flexibility in human resource management, and the use of accelerated procedures in procurement (Da Cruz & Marques, 2012). SoEs are often bounded by too many goals and, in practice, it is exceedingly difficult to replicate the discipline and performance of private companies (Da Cruz & Marques, 2012).

The opposite is represented by privatization, and in-between we have different forms of partnership, which can take the form of institutional PPP (joint venture/mixed companies) or contractual PPP/concession (CPPP).

As Rangan et al. (2006) explain in their study, when public benefits significantly exceed private benefits (e.g., a general interest service with no or low economic interest) but the public sector's costs are far higher than the private sector's costs (i.e., private actors hold higher expertise and they could be more efficient) then there is scope for public-private collaboration.

Both CPPP and institutional PPP involve delegated responsibility of production (operation), finance, and the collection of tariffs. In the first type of PPP, rights and obligations are regulated by a contract, while in the second, they are guaranteed by company statutes and by the shareholder agreement.

Mixed companies appear as an alternative both to pure public production and to the delegation of services to private firms through concession contracts. The mixed company model has been seen as a solution to long-term concession contracts, based on a "buyer-seller" type of cooperation, which generates significant transaction costs and relevant efforts in the design, monitoring, and enforcement of contracts, which have often resulted as being incomplete, especially for small to medium-sized municipalities that lack the resources and expertise needed to deal with specialists from the private sector. In this context, institutional PPP has been considered a valuable solution, able to regulate the partnership from within, with a relational (as opposite to contractual) approach to governance (Reeves, 2008). In the words of MacNeil (1974), in relational agreements, the "spirit of the contract" should prevail over the "letter of the contract."

However, the adoption of this model has shown some relevant drawbacks, due to the difficulties to embody two opposite goals under a single governance structure. As Laffont and Tirole (1991) wrote, "no man can serve two masters." In the same vein, Eckel and Vining (1985) found that mixed companies can result in the "worst of both worlds," where neither profitable nor social goals can be effectively achieved. This has been due to varied reasons, among them:

- the influence of politics in the appointment of board members, which may compromise a selection process based on ethical and professional standards (Marra, 2007);
- lack of clear and stable objectives (Boardman & Vining, 1989) which, in addition to the natural contradictory pressures within companies, can lead to a high degree of managerial "cognitive dissonance," a problem that may be accentuated in case of ownership dispersion, which is dominant in the public sector (i.e., the case of the public utility sector); and
- social goals are hard to determine, and social output is hard to measure, thus complicating any performance/benchmark review.

CPPP manages the balance between public goals and private profitability by leveraging on a system of complex and hard-to-design incentives, generally related to the capacity to achieve certain results and manage related risks. Also, CPPP generates mixed results, due to difficulties in the design of value for money and enforced contracts. CPPPs are analyzed in Chapter 6.

Lastly, there is the privatization option. Privatization can be referred to as an asset or, better and more often, as an SoE which manages the asset (see Box 5.1 which presents an example of privatization in Greece). The (full or partial) privatization of SoEs in charge of managing certain public services is a policy decision in search of more efficiency and more capital to be deployed in the expansion of a country's infrastructure network. However, the privatization of a company does not necessarily mean the privatization of the service/ assets. Here and quite often, a lot of confusion still exists also among sector experts and players. Once an SoE is privatized, it becomes a market player that competes in the market alongside other players that may enter, if suitable liberalization measures are introduced. However, many infrastructure sectors are natural monopolies and to achieve production efficiency, such markets should have a single operator. To foster efficiency and preserve public interest, monopolistic sectors require the intervention of a regulator. However, a single market operator can generate regulatory issues, due to information asymmetry, opportunism, and regulator capture. A common solution to the issue is competition in the market, where the right to operate a monopoly is subject to an auction, to allow the public sector to select the player on the basis of its capacity to maximize investment, efficiency, innovation, and service quality. The conditions of operation (rights and duties) are included in a written contract, leading to the term "regulation by contract." The modern version of this kind of relationship is labelled as concession/PPP (Marques & Berg, 2010).

BOX 5.1 THE PRIVATIZATION OF THE GREEK GAS GRID

After the 2007–2008 financial crisis, privatization was one of the main pillars of the Economic Adjustment Programme (2010–2018), the bailout plan set out by the European Commission, European Central Bank, and International Monetary Fund.[4] In reality, the privatization would generate revenue for debt repayment and fiscal recovery.

At the heart of this crucial effort is the Hellenic Republic Asset Development Fund (HRADF), which acts as a touchpoint for all parties interested in investing in Greece. HRADF was established in 2011 to promote and implement the Hellenic Republic privatization program, with the vision to deliver long-term, sustainable results for the economy and society. Currently, HRADF has sourced 25 percent of the total foreign direct investment attracted by Greece. To succeed in this crucial process, and therefore make the transaction appealing to international investors, HRADF is committed to a number of core principles, namely transparency and openness, adherence to international market standards during the tender processes, efficient corporate governance throughout the approval process, and the provision of high-quality services before and after the completion of any transaction.

The gas grid privatization program dates back to 2013, when, for geopolitical reasons, a Gazprom offer was withdrawn. In December 2019, a new international tender was launched to sell the shares of the three state-owned companies in charge of gas distribution (Eda Thess, Eda Attiki, and Deda). To support the process the shares were transferred into the DEPA infrastructure, owned by HRADF and Hellenic Petroleum S.A. At that time the DEPA infrastructure controlled 51 percent of EDA Thess, 100 percent of EDA Attikis, and 100 percent of DEDA.

In June 2020, after an assessment of prerequisites mainly focused on financial credentials, the list of preferred investors was made public. It consisted of the Consortium of Sino-Cee Fund & Shanghai Dazhong Public Utilities, EP Investment Advisors, First State Investments (European Diversified Infrastructure Fund II) Italgas SpA; KKR Global Infrastructure Investors III, and Macquarie (MEIF 6 DI Holdings). Five out of six preferred bidders were financial investors, and only Italgas, which is the third largest European gas distributor, was an industrial one.

The shortlisted investors had to perform their due diligence by July 2021, based on archival materials, face-to-face meetings with HRADF and its advisors, and site visits. The latter were needed to check the consistency of the pipelines.

During the tender process, the government amended the Energy Law to make the assets more appealing to private investors. Among others, the law dictated the opportunity to extend the length of the gas distribution concession from 20 to 30 years and state the rules to allow investors to buy 49 percent of Eda Thess.

After due diligence, in July 2021, only two of the preferred bidders, Italian Italgas and Czech EP Investment Advisors, submitted their final and best offers. The tender rules granted the seller the opportunity to ask for a better price from both bidders, or to the first one only in the case where the difference between the two offers would have been more than 15 percent.

In September 2021, Italgas was appointed as the final preferred investor, with a financial offer worth EUR 733 million. After checks by the Hellenic Court of Audit and the registration of Italgas as gas distributor in Greece, operated by the Regulatory Authority for Energy, the sales purchase agreement was signed.

The sale of state-owned gas distributors is crucial to introduce a system of concession-based "competition for the market" for the operation of the national gas grid, even though to make the deal interesting for investors, as written, the government decided to offer up the opportunity to extend the length of the gas grid concession. The privatization process makes it possible to not only increase revenues for the government, needed to meet fiscal targets set by the Troika,[5] but also to attract direct investment to improve the gas infrastructure. In reality, Italgas declared to invest around EUR 1.1 billion in the DEPA grid to expand it to 11,500 km by 2030 from the current 6,875 km. The deal is also expected to create additional business opportunities in fiberoptics and small-scale liquid natural gas development.

Therefore, privatization and PPP often co-exist across countries and industries, especially in some sectors, such as energy, telecommunications, and transport.

Indeed, it was and is still not rare to assist in a (whole or partial) sale of SoEs to private investors (to attract more capital, foster competition, and inject more efficiency), which then become potential concessionaires of public assets if they get a PPP contract awarded for the management of the asset (or in other terms, for the delivery of the service) or for expanding and managing the network. Of course, these dynamics are influenced by domestic regulations, some of which may create more favorable conditions to foster competition, as happens in the EU context.

In some contexts, we have also assisted in the so-called unbundling (separation) between the management of the main network infrastructure (which is generally a natural monopoly) and the delivery of the service to final users (by using the infrastructure) in order to foster competition (in the market), in sectors such as telecommunication, oil and gas, energy, and rail (the so-called "network industries"). The main network can be expanded/operated by an SoE (generally fully public or in any case under the full control of the public sector) or through a CPPP and the service by EOs that compete in the market, under the control of a regulator.

Such a framework, though generally referred to as economic infrastructure, can also be applied to social infrastructure, such as in healthcare, which is even more complex to analyze through an interpretative framework because of the vast differences across jurisdictions.

However, as discussed in Chapter 6, CPPP can be utilized for developing investments (hospitals or medical equipment) with or without the involvement of the EO in the delivery of clinical activities/services. The privatization option here is easier under an implementation perspective because there are no natural monopolies; however, it can have serious policy implications in the absence of a competent regulator. Indeed, privatization can take two forms, depending on who pays for the service: final users (full privatization) or single payer, which could be a government, in contexts where the service is paid via general taxation (such as in the context of a national health service) or via social security contributions (such as public or private insurance).

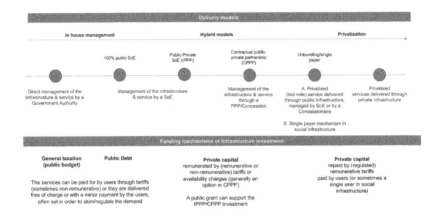

Figure 5.1   Infrastructure delivery models

Figure 5.1 shows in a comprehensive framework the models for the delivery of public interest services.

4.   MOBILIZING PRIVATE CAPITAL IN INFRASTRUCTURE

Total private investment in infrastructure[6] has increased over the past decade, both in the form of debt and equity. However, this increase has been mainly driven by secondary market transactions (i.e., the trading of existing infrastructure assets or refinancing).

Many nuances emerge in practice in private infrastructure financing. First of all, it is useful to make an initial distinction between the project finance approach and the corporate finance one. The former is the financing of the investment through a special purpose vehicle (SPV), purposely set up to attract dedicated capital for the development/expansion of infrastructure. The latter is the financing of the investment through the financial structure of the investor, typically a corporate one. The SPV is generally set up in greenfield PPP/concession contracts, whilst the corporate finance structure is applied for brownfield PPP/concession contracts, or in the case of an acquisition of a public company in a privatization process, to finance the development of the privatized asset. In corporate finance, we can also assist with some forms of project financing when the corporation issues, for example, a green bond to finance one or more projects with specific environmental goals.

The SPV is indeed a requirement in the case of a project financing debt structure because it ring-fences the cashflow generated by the project, which,

Table 5.1   *Main differences between corporate and project financing*

	Corporate financing	Project financing
Guarantees for financing	Assets of the borrower	Project assets
Effect on financial elasticity	Reduction of financial elasticity for the borrower	No or heavily reduced effect for sponsors
Accounting treatment	On-balance sheet	Off-balance sheet (the only effect will be either disbursement to subscribe equity in the SPV or for subordinated loans)
Main variables underlying the granting of financing	Solidity of balance sheet Profitability	Future cashflow
Degree of utilizable leverage	Depends on effects on borrower's balance sheet	Depends on cashflow generated by the project (leverage is usually much higher)

Source: Authors' elaboration, based on Gatti (2013).

in principle, is the main form of guarantee provided (Gatti, 2014), thus ensuring the provision of debt on a no- or limited-recourse basis. The assets of the SPV become collateral for the loans although they play a secondary role compared to project cashflow. This is in contrast to corporate finance where lenders rely on the borrower's creditworthiness for their loans. Furthermore, rights and obligations associated with an investment project are related to the SPV only.

For the reasons above, project financing is usually a much higher leveraged transaction compared to corporate financing. In a typical PPP project, up to 70–80 percent of financing is procured in the form of senior debt while the share of equity does not normally exceed 20–30 percent. A higher financial leverage allows for optimization of the cost of the overall financial structure. Table 5.1 provides an overview of the main differences between corporate and project financing.

 Going into more depth, taking the perspective of LTIs there are several different vehicles on offer for private investment in infrastructure with reference to equity (Figure 5.2a) and debt (Figure 5.2b). Equity can be invested by purchasing shares (directly, or by means of exchange traded funds) of public corporations investing in infrastructure (directly in projects, by providing capital to SPVs, or by purchasing shares in a company to be privatized); or by investing directly in unlisted SPVs or pooling capital in unlisted infrastructure funds, which can, in turn, invest in SPVs or in companies/assets under privatization. On the debt side, listed industrial players can issue regular or green bonds to develop infrastructure projects, or use them to buy company/assets under privatization; unlisted players generally borrow money in the form of loans

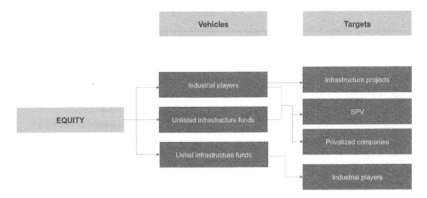

Figure 5.2a   Private capital investment mechanisms for infrastructure:
equity

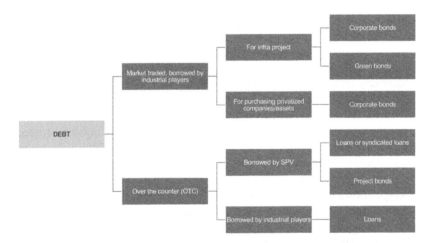

Figure 5.2b   Private capital investment mechanisms for infrastructure:
debt

which can be provided by commercial as well as development banks. SPVs, mainly involved in larger projects, get access to debt via syndicated project finance loans (provided by a pool of banks, headed by one or more mandated lead arranger) or by issuing project or green bonds.

Among the different instruments available, LTIs have traditionally invested in infrastructure through listed companies and fixed-income instruments (e.g., infrastructure exchange traded funds). It is only in the last two decades that they have started to recognize infrastructure as a distinct asset class and to hold the view that, while listed infrastructure tends to move in line with broader market trends, investing in unlisted infrastructure vehicles – although illiquid – can be beneficial for ensuring proper diversification and yield upside. Unlisted equity and debt funds are indeed typical "buy and hold" asset classes, suited to LTIs with a clear preference for stability – although they do not give exceptionally high returns.

In unlisted infrastructure lending, project bonds can play a significant role to attract LTIs in infrastructure, mainly after the completion of the risky construction phase. Compared to loans, project bonds are more standardized capital market instruments, with a higher degree of liquidity and a lower fixed-rate cost if the issue size is sufficiently large to generate enough liquidity in the secondary market, which makes them particularly attractive for LTIs.

While banks have traditionally been responsible for almost 90 percent of project finance loans, the relative share of bank finance to total unlisted infrastructure finance has decreased in recent years, with an increasing share of LTI finance, as bank lending has come under pressure following the Great Financial Crisis and the implementation of the Basel III regime (Financial Stability Board, 2018).

Banks will continue to play a significant role as lenders during the construction phase, considering their long-term expertise in infrastructure financing. Bank loans have several advantages vis-à-vis bonds to finance the construction phase, including:

• banks provide a fundamental screening and monitoring role as a watchdog; and
• infrastructure projects need a gradual disbursement of funds (the draw-down of debt is consistent with the implementation of work during the investment phase) and sometimes debt restructuring is needed to cope with project changes that may occur; bank lending offers such required flexibility.

Once the project moves into the operation phase (brownfield phase) and project risks are lower, loans can be refinanced with other capital market instruments, such as project bonds purchased by LTIs. This also allows banks to recycle capital to be invested in other greenfield projects.

Indeed, one of the main challenges in attracting LTIs to infrastructure is the level of risk that applies across the whole infrastructure lifecycle (Vecchi et al., 2017a). Among others, the most relevant are political and regulatory risks, construction and land expropriation risks, and demand risks. These risks are particularly applicable to greenfield projects in emerging economies, areas in which LTIs are more reluctant to invest.[7] Furthermore, infrastructure projects are hard to standardize because they are influenced by many context variables, and this increases the due diligence costs. For these reasons, LTIs prefer to invest in brownfield infrastructure or in privatized assets, by purchasing bonds issued for the refinancing of a senior loan provided during the construction phase.

To foster the attraction of capital in PPP/concession for greenfield project financing, governments keen to rely on LTIs have introduced specific policy measures to mitigate the risk profile of such projects. Such measures can be based on five different mechanisms (Gatti et al., 2019; Hellowell et al., 2014; Vecchi et al., 2017c), namely:

1. Grants, to reduce the capital requirements of the project, or to integrate revenues.
2. Availability-based payments, to neutralize the demand risk while leaving the performance risk with the private investor.
3. Credit-enhancement, such as the quite common "minimum payment guarantee," to reduce or cancel the credit default risk for lenders, i.e., either banks or (more specifically) project bondholders.
4. Direct provision of debt and equity capital by government, public financial agencies, or development banks, to offset the liquidity gap.
5. Other measures, among them, favorable taxation.

Table 5.2 presents the different alternatives to support LTI financing for infrastructure projects, and their effects on the main components of project capital structure and cashflow. Some of these measures can be considered a way to blend money at the project level, by acting on capital structure to increase the availability of capital and/or reduce the cost of the funding. Other measures instead are intended to provide support, by offering stabilization to project cashflow. Box 5.2 offers an overview of lending activities and guarantees provided by governments and government agencies, multilateral development banks (MDBs), development finance institutions, as well as other guarantee organizations to support infrastructure funding, in both developed and developing markets, alongside some examples of programs put in place by MDBs in emerging countries.

Furthermore, BF mechanisms, with structuring mechanisms explained in Chapter 4, have been introduced, especially by supranational institutions and development banks, to mobilize capital also at the system level. Box 5.3 describes the case of the securitization of a pool of project finance loans originated by the African Development Bank (AfDB) and purchased by LTIs, supported by mezzanine capital provided by public investors with a development mandate.

Table 5.2   *Main instruments to support capital attraction in (greenfield) PPP projects*

Measures	Features	Blending effect	Effects on capital structure/cashflow
Grant	Lump sum capital grant	Yes	Reducing the need for private capital
	Revenue grant: • periodic fixed amount (mitigating the demand risk) • revenue integration (it leaves the demand risk with the private player)	No	Increasing revenue volume and stability (when the EO retains the demand risk and tariffs are set at socially acceptable levels)
	Grant on debt interests	No	Decreasing the overall financial costs by reducing the amount of interest due to the debt provider (rarely used)
Availability payment	Availability payment is typical in the social infrastructure sector, where the main user is the public sector; in some cases, availability payment can be also used for economic infrastructure, in which case the service can be delivered free of charge to users, or tariffs are collected by the public authority	No	Eliminating the demand risk; ensuring revenue stability

Public-private collaborations for long-term investments

Measures	Features	Blending effect	Effects on capital structure/cashflow
Guarantee on debt	Minimum revenue guarantee, to guarantee a minimum level of revenues (generally those necessary to cover the debt service at some level of debt service coverage ratio (DSCR))	No	Mitigating the demand risk; increasing the revenue volume and stability
	Guarantee in case of default, to cover the payment of outstanding debt (both principal and interest) in the case of a private player's default	Yes	Providing credit enhancement; increasing the overall available funding, and/or reducing the interest rate applied on the debt
	Guarantee in case of refinancing, which repays lenders if the SPV fails to refinance the loan at maturity. In fact, in the context of mini perm (i.e., a debt structure that can ("soft" mini perm) or must ("hard" mini perm) be refinanced after the construction phase) there is a risk that existing debt will not be repaid from new borrowing (risk of refinancing), especially in the case of increased interest rates or adversely changed market conditions	Yes	Providing credit enhancement; increasing the overall available funding, and/or reducing the interest rate applied on the debt

Measures	Features	Blending effect	Effects on capital structure/cashflow
Provision of capital	Subordinated (junior) debt	Yes	Enhancing the credit quality of the senior debt; increasing the overall available funding, and/or reducing the interest rate applied on the senior debt
	Debt: • pari passu condition • at lower interest rate (concessional money)	Yes	Providing debt capital at competitive market conditions; in some circumstances, it can also be provided at lower rates, thus helping the project to meet the expectations of other debt capital investors, in terms of interest rates, DSCR, and maturity
	Equity: • at market conditions • at more advantageous conditions (concessional money)	Yes	Providing equity to fill the equity gap; reducing financial leverage, and therefore the exposure to credit risk; offering downside protection or upside leverage to private equity holders
Other measures	Favorable taxation: • favorable taxation schemes for SPV • favorable taxation schemes for equity investors	No	Introducing lower corporate taxation to sustain general viability of the project (i.e., increasing the free cashflow from operations); introducing lower taxation on "qualified dividends" and long-term capital gains to attract equity investors

BOX 5.2   AN OVERVIEW OF MULTILATERAL
           DEVELOPMENT LENDING AND
           GUARANTEES TO INFRASTRUCTURE

Direct lending and guarantees provided by governments, MDBs and development finance institutions are important instruments to expand infrastructure financing at the project level, especially in developing countries.

Examples of programs to attract LTIs and support infrastructure financing implemented by MDBs include the Fondo Nacional de Infraestructura
(FONADIN), a fund created by the Mexican government within Banobras,
the largest MDB of Mexico, and the Credit Guarantee and Investment
Facility (CGIF), established by the ten members of ASEAN together with
the People's Republic of China, Japan, Republic of Korea, and the Asian
Development Bank.

FONADIN provides financial guarantees to both Mexican states and municipalities that are keen to implement infrastructure-based PPP, as well
as directly to infrastructure projects. They are designed to enhance private
participation in the financing of infrastructure and they include:

- Securities debt guarantees: these guarantees can be used to support
  bonds issued to the market by project developers.
- Bank guarantees: these guarantees support the debt service the project
  must pay to a bank due to contracted loans.
- Guarantees for service provision projects: these guarantees are intended
  to cover the periodic payment obligations of the contracting units
  derived from the service provision contracts signed with the suppliers
  of the service.
- Pari passu guarantees are other similar schemes with the main difference
  that losses are assumed pro rata between BANOBRAS and commercial
  banks.

FONADIN also supports medium-sized Mexican concessionaires in the energy and construction sector through equity investments, with the aim to
help them compete with international or larger sponsors.

CGIF is part of the Asian Bond Markets Initiative and serves to provide
credit guarantees for local currency denominated bonds issued by companies
(including SPVs for the development of infrastructure) in ASEAN+3 countries. CGIF offers construction period guarantees to issuers of project bonds
and secures the completion of construction works and the commencement
of operations of greenfield infrastructure projects. If the construction phase
is not successfully completed, CGIF reimburses bondholders all amounts
owned by SPVs. Due to CGIF's due diligence process in the course of pro-

viding the guarantee, investors are assured that construction risks are well assessed and covered.

BOX 5.3 CAPITAL RELIEF AND BLENDING MECHANISMS FOR EXPANDING INFRASTRUCTURE LENDING IN AFRICA

A project finance securitization is a transaction that involves repackaging the risk of a portfolio of project finance loans for infrastructure development. With securitizations, LTIs participate in a pool of loans (in other words, financing the infrastructure project only indirectly) originated by a bank. From an institutional investor's perspective, the advantage of this model is that these kinds of loans structured as bonds can be tailored to specific needs and can benefit from a diversified default risk. From a bank's perspective, by moving project finance loans from the bank's balance sheets and transferring the credit risk of the underlying loan portfolio to LTIs via securitization, it accelerates loan issuance and frees up bank-lending capacity (i.e., asset recycling), thereby expanding overall lending to infrastructure.

A promising application of securitization has been the AfDB Room-to-Run, the first portfolio securitization between an MDB and private investors closed in September 2018. The purpose of the Room-to-Run transaction was to enable the AfDB to expand lending capacity, redeploying freed-up capital in renewable energy projects across the African continent without requiring supplementary capital from shareholder governments.

The reference portfolio pooled by AfDB consisted of 45 seasoned loans, denominated in multiple currencies, to power and transportation infrastructure in North Africa, West Africa, Central Africa, East Africa, and Southern Africa. As shown in Figure 5.3, the transaction was structured into four different tranches: a senior tranche worth USD 727.5 million, a senior mezzanine tranche worth USD 100 million, a mezzanine tranche worth USD 152.5 million, and a junior tranche worth USD 20 million. While AfDB provided first-loss capital by retaining the junior tranche, Africa50, the pan-African infrastructure investment platform established by African governments alongside AfDB, invested in the mezzanine tranche. In addition, the European Commission provided supplementary credit protection through the European Fund for Sustainable Development by investing in the senior mezzanine tranche.

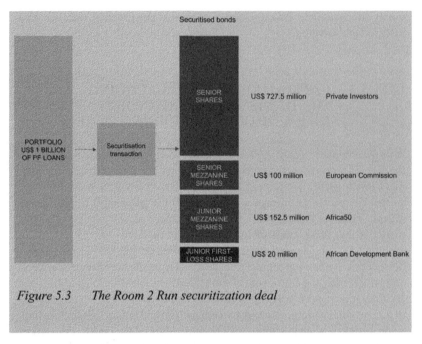

Figure 5.3   The Room 2 Run securitization deal

The project de-risking measures are not alternatives to BF mechanisms, since they offer support to specific projects and, therefore, can be combined with blended mechanisms to sustain a stable capital attraction. Such measures and BF mechanisms are salient to attract LTIs but must be designed to prevent situations of moral hazard. Any form of guarantee that limits the construction risk can seriously reduce the incentives to deliver the infrastructure on time and on budget and, at the same time, generate public debt. In this context, the role of development banks can be fundamental in crafting balanced measures and in supporting governments in developing a feasible project pipeline and strengthening the applicable legal framework. With regards to the need for mitigation of the demand risk, the use of availability charge payments, especially in economic infrastructure, could be a useful solution, as experienced in Europe after the financial crisis (Vecchi et al., 2015). Its effects are much more controllable in respect to a minimum revenue guarantee, which can expose governments to an unpredictable disbursement of money to top up the missing revenue. Alternatively, the competent authority could use it during the ramp-up period, keeping the option to switch it to regular toll-based payments, cashed in by the concessionaire when the demand becomes more stable and mature.

More in general, when a project is heavily supported by public funds or guarantees, EOs may have low or no incentive to:

- form optimal bidding consortia;
- undertake careful and reliable assessments of the project's features (e.g., capital, operational costs, and demand); or
- select the best contractors and ensure the project's overall efficiency.

In other words, public guarantees can undermine EO incentives to identify, monitor, and minimize project risks and thereby generate substantial additional fiscal burden for governments and taxpayers.

NOTES

1. For a review of the impact of Covid-19 on infrastructure needs, see: OECD, Covid-19 and a New Resilient Infrastructure Landscape, February 22, 2021. Available at: www.oecd.org/coronavirus/policy-responses/covid-19-and-a-new -resilient-infrastructure-landscape-d40a19e3/, accessed March 14, 2022.
2. Economic infrastructure is defined as the assets that enable society and the economy to function, such as transport (airports, ports, roads, and railroads), energy (gas and electricity), water and waste, and telecommunications facilities. Social infrastructure is the long-term physical asset that facilitates social services and includes schools, universities, hospitals, prisons, and community housing, which ameliorate human development, quality of life, and living standards.
3. Research financed by the EIB STARBEI program, with the aim of adding further evidence to the results exposed in the 2017 Report of the High-Level Task Force on Investing in Social Infrastructure.
4. This case was written thanks to the support of Paolo Gallo and Nunzio Ferulli, respectively CEO and Head of Public Affairs, Italgas spa.
5. European troika is a term used, especially in the media, to refer to the decision group formed by the European Commission, the European Central Bank, and the International Monetary Fund. The usage arose in the context of the "bailouts" of Cyprus, Greece, Ireland, and Portugal necessitated by their prospective insolvency caused by the world financial crisis of 2007–2008.
6. Data regarding the involvement of the private sector in infrastructure suffer from some interpretation bias; when we talk about private infrastructure financing it is worth clarifying that PPP are not equivalent to the privatization of infrastructure or related services.
7. In 2020, 85 percent of total capital committed to unlisted infrastructure focused on developed markets, for their more stable political and regulatory environment. Furthermore, out of 90 pension funds investing in infrastructure surveyed by the OECD, only 17 were keen to invest in greenfield projects, while the rest invested only in brownfield projects. See Unlisted Infrastructure Fundraising, Preqin; Annual Survey of Large Pension Funds and Public Pension Reserve Funds, OECD.

6.   Developing infrastructure through contractual public-private partnership

1.   PUBLIC-PRIVATE PARTNERSHIPS VERSUS CONCESSION: TWO TERMS NOW RECONCILED

At the very beginning, the word public-private partnership was used to refer to contracts where paymentsw to EOs came from the public authority.[1] Such contracts were introduced for social infrastructure (such as hospitals, schools, prisons, but also federal buildings), with services typically funded with general taxation and therefore delivered free of charge to citizens, in the Anglo-Saxon context, and especially in the UK, Australia, and Canada, where we assisted the first conceptualizations and applications of the New Public Management theories. Since there was no revenue flow generated by users, because the core services (i.e., education, clinical treatments) were delivered directly by the competent authority, the remuneration of the EO (for investments and non-core services) came from the payment of an availability charge by the authority itself, set to repay the investment and the delivery of ancillary non-core services (i.e., cleaning, catering, portering, etc.).

At that time, the word concession was mainly used to refer to greenfield or brownfield projects for the building of new, or the expansion and then the management of, economic infrastructure (in transport, oil and gas, telecommunications, etc.), with users paying a fee for the use.

In more recent years, the availability payment, born in the context of social infrastructure, has become increasingly frequent for economic infrastructure, considering that the demand risk for greenfield projects is difficult to predict and for private investors to influence (see Chapter 5).

Nowadays, the distinction between PPP and concession is no longer relevant; however, it still creates confusion. Both terminologies can co-exist, since the term "concession" has a legal nature, while the term PPP has a more generic meaning.

From a legal perspective, at least in the legal framework of the EU, which is one of the most advanced globally, since a PPP contract is based on a risk allocation principle, it can be considered a concession contract, which is characterized by the allocation of the so-called operative risk to EOs, contrary to traditional procurement.

Directive 2014/23/EU states:

the definition of concession should be clarified, in particular by referring to the concept of operating risk. The main feature of a concession, the right to exploit the works or services, always implies the transfer to the concessionaire of an operating risk of economic nature involving the possibility that it will not recoup the investments made and the costs incurred in operating the works or services awarded under normal operating conditions even if a part of the risk remains with the contracting authority or contracting entity. (Considerandum 18)

An operating risk should stem from factors which are outside the control of the parties. Risks such as those linked to bad management, contractual defaults by the economic operator or to instances of force majeure are not decisive for the purpose of classification as a concession, since those risks are inherent in every contract, whether it be a public procurement contract or a concession. An operating risk should be understood as the risk of exposure to the vagaries of the market, which may consist of either a demand risk or a supply risk, or both a demand and supply risk. Demand risk is to be understood as the risk on actual demand for the works or services which are the object of the contract. Supply risk is to be understood as the risk on the provision of the works or services which are the object of the contract, in particular the risk that the provision of the services will not match demand. (Considerandum 20)

2.   THE ESSENCE OF A CONTRACTUAL PUBLIC-PRIVATE PARTNERSHIP

A PPP is a long-term contract between a public authority and, usually, an SPV, in order to design, build, finance, maintain, and operate economic or social infrastructure.[2]

A PPP contract for infrastructure and service delivery is characterized by at least the following features:

- mid-/long-term agreement;
- investment of private capital on an exclusive basis or with a co-investment of public money;
- risk allocation between public and private parties; and
- performance-related pay (i.e., based on results or outcome).

SPVs are generally set up to ring-fence project risks and cashflow, thus fostering the attraction of capital.

Two kinds of private sponsors are involved in PPP transactions:

1. pure financial investors, i.e., those investing their capital (in the form of equity and shareholder loans) in the SPV; and
2. industrial investors.

The latter generally invest money in the SPV and are entrusted by the SPV, through subcontracts, to build the infrastructure and/or operate and manage the underlying services. Indeed, industrial players invest in the SPV's equity to expand their business and to gain access to better economic conditions for subcontracted activities. The SPV may use subcontractors different from the players that are also industrial investors. It is widespread for industrial sponsors that are subcontractors to further subcontract a part of the activities assigned by the SPV.

In sectors where PPP contracts are applied as a standard way to deliver public services, the involved EOs are usually large industrial companies, often listed, who may decide not to establish an SPV. However, we are also assisting in such contexts to an expanding role of infrastructure funds, which may run the contract on their own, by subcontracting tasks to industrial players, or through joint ventures (and therefore SPV) with industrial players. In general, infrastructure funds invest on their own when industrial/construction risks are limited and therefore well predictable.

A PPP contract for greenfield projects is generally financed through a project finance scheme, where a large portion of the investment is financed with debt in the form of syndicated loans or bonds. When PPP is used for brownfield projects, such as the expansion/maintenance of the network and the delivery of the service, capital is deployed by the EO player, generally a listed company, with a corporate finance model. More details on the features of financial structures are provided in Chapter 5. Figure 6.1 shows the typical structure of a CPPP.

3.   RISK ALLOCATION

Under the perspective of public authorities, sound risk allocation is the main advantage of a PPP contract, and is its main feature, compared to traditional procurement. Without balanced risk allocation, whereby the appropriate risks are transferred to the private partner, there is no incentive to achieve the expected performance targets in terms of efficiency (on time, on budget) and efficiency/effectiveness (on quality). Risk allocation is based on two essential elements, namely a robust and complete set of contract clauses and an accurate design of the payment mechanism, which must be able to incentivize EOs/SPVs to take on full responsibility for the risks transferred to them, by endeavoring to manage contract performance to minimize the occurrence of such risks, or to mitigate their consequences. If the cost associated with the occurrence of harmful events is higher than the cost needed to avoid it, the EO/SPV will be likely to implement all possible counter-measures in order to prevent them from happening or to ensure their consequences are mitigated. If

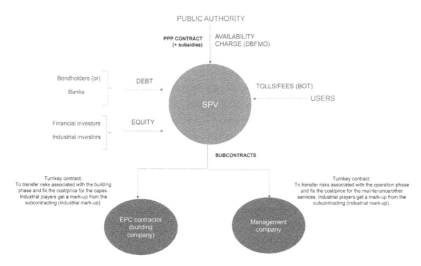

Figure 6.1   The typical structure of a contractual public-private partnership

input data in the financial plan are fully risk adjusted, risk allocation is jeopardized because the occurrence of risk would not have a significant impact on the project returns. In other words, the EO/SPV has no incentive to monitor, manage, or mitigate risks. This is especially true in availability-based contracts or in user fee-based PPP with a rigid demand, i.e., when revenue is almost fixed.

Risks in PPP can be classified on the basis of their specific nature: political and regulatory; market or external; or technical.

- Political and regulatory risks depend on the activities of the state at various levels of governance. They may arise, for example, from planning changes, legal changes, or changes in government policy that may threaten the interests of project stakeholders. Often, political risk relates to government action at the central or regional levels. In some cases, this type of risk emerges from the behavior of the CA itself. These risks must always be retained by CAs.
- Macro-economic and market risks arise from the possibility that the economic environment and the market may change over time. These risks must be carefully analyzed with reference to the specific context: in some cases, they can be transferred to EOs/SPVs; in other cases they must be retained by CAs. They require a sophisticated case-by-case evaluation. In the case of an SPV, if it retains such macro-economic risks, it tends to transfer them

to its subcontractors, via a pass-through mechanism, in order to de-risk itself as much as possible and therefore attract financial investors.

- Technical risks are linked to the EO/SPV's know-how and the features of the project and technology. They are generally retained by the EO or by subcontractors of SPVs (via a pass-through mechanism) and they include:
  - the risk that design/engineering processes fail to perform as expected;
  - the risk of faulty building techniques or higher costs in construction;
  - the risk that maintenance/service costs are higher than projected; and
  - the risk that maintenance/service delivery does not meet the standard required under the contract, thus generating additional costs.

The two main relevant risks borne by investors are the construction and the demand risk. The latter is discussed Section 4.

The construction – or investment – risk happens when the following elements apply:

- a challenging investment schedule is in place or, at least, no relief measure (for instance, extension of the contract duration) is provided in the event of late completion thereof;
- the contract provides that delays in the delivery of the investment entail a correspondent reduction of the operational phase, thus automatically reducing the volume of revenue and therefore the project return;
- any extra investment cost is intended to be borne by EOs/SPVs; and
- the need to increase or change the period of investment in technological updates.

Investment risk also includes risk linked to increases in the cost of financing, compared to the forecasts encompassed in the financial plan. This risk is generally mitigated by the SPV by borrowing money at a fixed interest rate or by hedging the cost of the debt, the risk of increased financial costs.

Furthermore, inflation is a relevant macro-economic risk to be carefully considered. When structuring the payment mechanism of PPP contracts of any kind, indexation to the inflation rate is always a critical element to carefully consider. Indexation is important in long-term contracts in order to ensure revenue maintains the purchasing power needed to cover operating costs throughout their entire duration. However, when the project involves significant investment, the majority of revenue is committed to covering capital expenses and the cost of debt, which, as a general rule, are both fixed. Investment costs included in the financial plan may already incorporate estimated inflation, at least in mature economies where inflation is quite stable and predictable. Therefore, only the part of revenue intended to cover operating costs and equity remuneration should be linked to inflation. Inflation assumptions incorporated into the financial plan of the project might result in being quite different from actual inflation, used to index tolls and availability payments during contract execution. In this context, if the entire revenue provided for in the contract is linked to inflation, project returns may change significantly, thus exposing both parties to a risk that they cannot control. If actual inflation is lower than predicted, revenue will grow at a slower pace, thus generating a contraction of the return; if, on the contrary, actual inflation is higher than predicted, revenue will grow more rapidly, thus generating a higher profitability. By reducing the amount of revenue linked to inflation, a higher portion thereof has to be forecasted in the financial plan, at least in the initial years of the management phase. This can be a critical issue; however, partial indexation is fundamental in order to reduce the return volatility, thereby limiting the risk of contract renegotiation. Furthermore, the suggested approach is useful to reduce the overall amount of revenue needed to secure the target return, improving the value for money (VfM) for taxpayers and the affordability of availability-based PPP for CAs.

4. USER-BASED PUBLIC-PRIVATE PARTNERSHIP AND THE DEMAND RISK

User-based PPP and availability-based PPP are two of the main payment mechanisms applied in PPP schemes, as briefly introduced above.

The typical one is based on tariffs paid by users, and it is common in economic infrastructure.

It is worth noting that this type of infrastructure is called economic because it can be economically exploited: in other words, it can be used to deliver services paid by end users, through tariffs, which remunerate private investment.

In such contracts, since the only source of revenue consists of tariffs paid by end users, EOs/SPVs bear all or most of the demand risks, although such risks may be mitigated by the CA through various types of guarantees, such as minimum revenue guarantee, as discussed in Chapter 5.

This type of contract faces some critical issues, especially when applied to greenfield infrastructure, where demand can be difficult to forecast. The unpredictability of demand can affect the feasibility and bankability of the project. Demand risk is easier to estimate in brownfield projects. Unpredictable demand may have a lesser impact on projects with minor investment components, where the main goal of PPP contracts is the delivery of intangible services. In this case, tariffs are mainly meant for remuneration of operational costs.

When demand is difficult to estimate, it is advisable to structure PPP contracts relying on availability charges, whereby the demand risk is retained by CAs. The latter can use the tariffs collected (often by the SPV) to fund availability payments. After the so-called ramp-up phase, i.e., a transition period after the construction phase, as soon as revenue is more stable and it is possible to establish demand trends through a statistical method based on historical series, the payment mechanism can be switched to a tariff regime. At this stage, in general, demand is more predictable and, therefore, relative risks are quite similar to brownfield projects. The choice of basing PPP contracts on availability payments is further justified by considering that, in a well-structured contract, only those risks that can be controlled and influenced by EOs/SPVs should be transferred to them. Indeed, for large infrastructure, especially when greenfield, not only is demand difficult to estimate but also it cannot be easily influenced by EOs/SPVs through its management activities because it mainly depends on macro-economic and social factors.

When availability charge is applied, it is fundamental to ensure other risks, such as construction and service performance, are appropriately allocated. To this end, adequate deductions and/or penalties should be applied to the availability payment when service standards are not met, from a quantitative and/or qualitative standpoint. However, sound contract monitoring, based on key performance indicators, should also be put in place when the payment mechanism is based on tariffs, charged directly to end users, since a lot of economic infrastructure has a rigid demand, due to the characteristics as a natural monopoly. In these instances, the quality of service does not drive the demand and EOs may fail to deliver the expected quality with a potentially lower effect on the project revenue.

The payment to the EO/SPV may also be shaped as a shadow toll, whereby CAs pay EOs/SPVs per each single user, without effectively charging end users. However, this form of payment does not address the lack of predictability of the demand since demand risk is in any case retained by EOs/SPVs. This form of indirect tolling is, therefore, chosen for policy reasons by those authorities who are willing to allow end users access to relevant infrastructure and services free of charge. The shadow toll system has mostly been applied to transport infrastructure projects.

Demand forecast is even more difficult in emerging countries, where people are not used to paying a fee for services and the majority of the population may prefer to continue to use old infrastructure; this is quite common for transport infrastructure. In such contexts, CAs may choose to apply lower tariffs to accustom people progressively to paying tariffs. Such choice entails the need for CAs to integrate EOs/SPVs revenue from fees with additional resources collected through general taxation.

When demand is difficult to estimate, the use of a revenue-sharing mechanism is another option to consider. This is usually applied when revenue is generous and forecasted returns of the project are likely to be higher than the optimal level of return as predetermined on the basis of the level of transferred risks. In the case of hard-to-predict demand, CAs can choose to structure a PPP contract based on a conservative estimate of demand and to support it with a capital grant. In such cases, including a revenue-sharing mechanism in the contract allows for adjustment should revenue increase to a level above the set ceiling, by "clawing back" the excess, thus generating a sort of "remuneration" of the initial grant paid by CAs. The revenue-sharing mechanism should be triggered by increased revenue above a certain level, to be defined prior to the awarding procedure or the closing of the contract, on the basis of a sensitivity analysis of the financial plan. In such cases, it is fundamental to put in place a transparent mechanism of revenue/demand monitoring. Sometimes, CAs are not keen on granting revenue or capital contributions or tariff integrations to EOs/SPVs, for budgetary constraints or for fear of sanctions from audit authorities, thus preferring to extend contract duration. However, this approach is wrong since it is not based on solid financial evaluations. When the gross margin (i.e., the difference between revenue and operational expenses) of a PPP project is limited, the achievement of financial equilibrium would, in fact, require an excessive extension of the contract duration, which, in turn, may provoke a de facto monopoly. Furthermore, an abnormally long contract duration would not be consistent with the average length of financial contracts, which is generally set between 10 to 20 years. A longer maturity period is only possible where a development bank is part of the financial jigsaw of the deal. Therefore, the need to match contract duration with debt maturity requires entering a debt renegotiation: this is a risk EOs/SPVs are rarely willing to bear.

The availability payment could be a preferable option when CAs are willing to promote equity, through generalized and equal access to critical services and a remunerative tariff, i.e., a tariff covering operational cost, capital cost, and the cost of financial resources invested by EOs/SPVs, may not be affordable by end users. In cases in which CAs decide to provide social tariffs for some categories of users, such as the young or the elderly, sometimes associated with specific service requirements (for example, in sports facilities CAs often require services and tariffs to be set so as to encourage certain categories of users, such as students or sports associations), a revenue integration could be a sound option. Revenue integration mechanisms should be adequately crafted. Such mechanisms may be based on tariff integrations – i.e., an integration for each tariff paid by specific categories of end users in order to reach the level of remuneration needed for the project to be sustainable – thus leaving demand risk with EOs/SPVs, or it can take the form of a fixed revenue integration to be calculated on the basis of the financial plan. The latter solution should be preferred when specific policy goals heavily influence the revenue structure, thus limiting EOs/SPVs' room for maneuver.

Lastly, CAs may opt to allow EOs/SPVs access to commercial revenue in order to sustain an infrastructure project with a weak demand. Such a solution should be carefully explored since it may increase the complexity of the project, thus requiring the execution of the contract by a consortium of EOs with multiple competencies.

5.   AVAILABILITY-BASED PUBLIC-PRIVATE PARTNERSHIP

As already mentioned, availability-based PPP – setting aside the above suggestions regarding economic infrastructure in cases where demand is unpredictable or greatly impacted by policy choices – are usually appropriate for projects aimed at delivering:

1. Infrastructure or investments needed for the delivery of services directly operated by public authorities, as may be the case for some critical services, such as health or education; these are also considered merit goods, i.e., services ensuring great public benefits and, therefore, are generally funded with general taxation, especially because tariffs may not be affordable for the majority of the population.
2. General public services, when tariffs cannot be applied because they are provided on a communal basis, as opposed to services provided to a specific target of users (for this reason general public services are considered public goods, which are defined by the economic theory as non-excludable and non-rivalrous); these are, therefore, funded by general taxation, such as street lighting or urban facility management.
3. Infrastructure used by public authorities (office buildings or facilities in the defense sector).
4. Non-core services bought by authorities, such as in the case of energy efficiency projects in public building or street lighting or investments to make urban areas smarter (smart cities).

In such transactions, EOs/SPVs are in charge of the design, financing, and building of infrastructure and the delivery of so-called non-core services. The availability charge is set so as to ensure the remuneration of operational costs, capital costs, and costs of the private capital invested. Payment of the availability charge is ensured by CAs through public resources deriving from general taxation.

When PPP contracts involve infrastructure for the delivery of merit goods, such as schools and hospitals, availability charges generally ensure the remuneration of investment and infrastructure maintenance (hard-facility management costs); all other possible services to be included in the contract are usually paid via specific tariffs, sometimes even based on consumption, though minimum quantities are generally provided for in the contract.

In such cases, it is advisable to avoid extending the scope of contracts by including too many services, and a light model should be preferred in order to avoid excessive complexity. This is even more the case as non-core services tend to evolve rapidly and their quick evolution is difficult to contractualize while maintaining balanced risk allocation. In emerging countries, however, the main trend is to include many non-core services in the scope of the contract, aspiring to reach wider or even complete outsourcing. This approach is based on the assumption that private players should be more efficient than the public sector or to avoid multiple awarding procedures, which are expensive, time consuming, and risky, especially in terms of litigation. EOs/SPVs' efficiency can be captured also by traditional, though sophisticated, contracts, while transaction costs associated with the management of such contracts are no higher than those associated with the effective management of complex PPP contracts. Therefore, the features of the contract and, especially, the services to be included therein, must be carefully considered and designed ex ante since avoiding any misconceived emulation effect is of the essence. An important lesson to be learned is that the institutional and regulatory framework, as well as factual circumstances, does matter and although a contract model may work in one jurisdiction, this may not be true in another.

An effective payment mechanism should be conceived as follows:

Availability payment: investment component (capex + cost of the capital) + maintenance component + service fees (if further services are included).

The investment component remunerates capital expenses (capex), such as design and construction costs, and the cost of capital (debt and equity). Therefore, the actual amount of the availability payment depends on the volume of investments and duration of the contract since its aim is to achieve economic and financial equilibrium.

Availability payment mechanisms should be associated with an adequate system of deductions and penalties in case the EO/SPV should not be able to deliver the predefined level of availability of the facilities or meet the quality standards for services. A sound mechanism of deductions for the availability payment should be based on two different levels, i.e., a minimum and an average one. Therefore, for each of the main areas of the facility involved, the contract should include minimum and average indicators, thus allowing for a granular definition of the meaning of availability and, therefore, the application of deductions/penalties. The system could, for instance, be designed in the following way:

• if the EO/SPV meets the average parameters, no deductions are applied;

- if the availability falls between the minimum and the average levels, to be detected and measured for each single indicator, deductions associated with each of such indicators can be applied only to the maintenance/service component of the payment; and
- if the availability further falls below the minimum target, then deductions may also affect the investment component, thus resulting in an actual reduction of the return.

When other non-core services are included, specific key performance indicators and deductions should be applied to service fees. It is important that the amount of the deduction creates incentives for EOs/SPVs to foster sound management of the contract. In fact, if deductions are too low, EOs/SPVs have no incentive to put in place all the measures to avoid underperformance, because the impact of deductions/penalties on their return is lower than the cost involved in delivering the expected standards. In some cases, it may be useful for CAs to calculate the social costs generated by disruption in the availability of the facility or services: this could be a good benchmark in order to identify the appropriate level of applicable deductions/penalties.

6.   PUBLIC-PRIVATE PARTNERSHIP FOR SOCIAL INVESTMENTS: FOCUS ON HEALTHCARE

If the application of PPP is quite straightforward in economic infrastructure, where the concession model has become part of a standard way to deliver, its use for social infrastructure, where the investment gap is relevant, is still critical. First of all, the delivery models applied to social infrastructure/services are quite different across the world and they are massively influenced by specific institutional and governance settings. Second, the involvement of private investors has been perceived as a politically sensitive issue in sectors such as healthcare and education.[3]

However, it is worth recalling that a PPP is not privatization, and the role of the private sector can be limited and, in any case, controlled under strong public governance. Therefore, the risk that a PPP could become de facto privatization can be eliminated.

In order to support investors to understand the main approaches that can be used in the healthcare sector, despite country-specific features, it is possible to refer to three main models of PPP, which have emerged in the last 20 years. The first two can also represent reference schemes for the education sector where, in general, upfront investment may be lower compared to the health sector. In both, outcome-based contracts can also be applied, and especially in education. Outcome-based contracts are explained in Chapter 3.

The most important model in use in healthcare is the so-called availability-based contract (DBFMO). It is the reference model in countries where healthcare is managed through a national healthcare service (paid with general taxation), such as in Anglo-Saxon countries (UK, Canada, and Australia), and also in continental Europe, especially Italy, Spain, and Portugal. It follows the scheme explained in Section 5. At the beginning contracts included many non-clinical services; in recent years, a new model is emerging, the so-called PPP light (Vecchi et al., 2020), where, during operation, only hard-facility management services are included (maintenance and energy management). This model should be useful to overcome the rigidity of traditional all-inclusive contracts and to achieve better VfM.

The availability-based model is appropriate for mature economies where the need of governments is purely to accelerate the modernization of the network of healthcare facilities, by transferring the on-time, on-budget, and on-quality risks to the EOs/SPVs. Another advantage can be found in the opportunity to ensure appropriate maintenance of facilities; in the context of curtailed budgets, not only is the initial investment financing critical but also the allocation of budget for maintenance, thus causing a rapid obsolescence of facilities.

In emerging countries, with weak healthcare systems and large parts of the population left without coverage of fundamental services, an appropriate model can be the so-called "clinic." Differently from the DBFMO, here the EO/SPV is not only involved in building and running the facilities but also in the delivery of all clinical activities. Even though clinical activities are managed by the private operator, it is different from the accreditation model, where the government only sets minimum delivery standards and reimburses the operator with a system of tariffs, called diagnostic related groups. This model can be dangerous because it may generate an over-remuneration of EOs if they stimulate an unnecessary demand; or it may leave certain more complex (and expensive) pathologies uncovered if tariffs are not remunerative.

In the clinic model, in principle such risks can be avoided, but of course only if the contract is well structured and the public governance is strong enough. If the first element is addressed thanks also to the support of development banks, the second remains critical, especially in emerging countries. However, under weak public governance a traditional model may also fail, and weak governance can't stand as an excuse for non-adoption of the PPP model. It must be addressed as a precondition to support inclusive development.

In the clinic model, two possible payment mechanisms can be used:

- Capitation fee (fee per person living in the catchment area of the hospital); as in the accreditation model, it may generate a negative selection of cases (with no coverage of cronicities).

- Availability fee, defined based on a certain basket of services, based on the health condition of the population; the fee can be difficult to define if there is no past track record (e.g., Lesotho experienced an explosion of demand and an unpredictable increase of the fee due to its EO, as reported by Vecchi & Hellowell (2018)).

A third model of PPP is the technological PPP, also known as medical equipment service (MES). The contract is aimed at providing medical equipment and includes at least full risk maintenance. It may also include a technological refresh, though this is difficult to manage especially when the public sector is weak, due to the unpredictability of technology and associated prices and future clinical needs. In some cases, it can include medical staff, especially when applied in emerging countries. It is also very much used in private hospitals, and can be incorporated within both a DBFMO and a clinic model. There are two possible payment mechanisms and these can be used on their own or together:

- a tariff per use paid by the public hospital; and
- an availability fee.

MES contracts are used to accelerate the modernization of healthcare technology of an entire hospital, a network of public hospitals, or a single department. Due to the relatively low upfront capital, a MES is generally developed directly by industrial players operating in the field or by independent vendors. The attraction of LTInv in such contracts implies the need to extend the MES contract to a network of hospitals or, otherwise, for investors to create portfolios of MESs. The latter may be expensive and not consistent with their investment period, because it can be subject to a risk of delays by competent authorities in setting up a consistent pipeline of contracts.

7.   A RENEWED APPROACH TO PUBLIC-PRIVATE PARTNERSHIP

The popularity of PPP is associated with macro-economic arguments, i.e., closing the infrastructure gap in context with a lack of public funds (from taxation or public debt). Indeed, it has been and is still considered by governments as a way to account for the asset off-balance sheet.

However, PPP contracts can also act as a filter, especially for user fee-based projects, by skimming unfeasible and unbankable projects. This is particularly true for projects only partially funded or guaranteed by the public sector.

A second approach to PPP is driven by micro-economic arguments. On the one hand, there is the opportunity to deliver infrastructure on time, on budget, and on quality, thanks to the incentives set by the contract to private investors. This is known as the VfM dimension of PPP contracts. On the other hand, PPP can be an extraordinary opportunity to attract the competence and innovation capacity of the private sector, by also drawing on its refocus on the environment and society, to achieve superior goals and outcomes otherwise not possible with a traditional approach, especially when the investors are also paid on the basis of the societal or public value achieved. This can be called value for people (VfP).

Despite the fact that CPPP are not a new concept, high barriers still exist which prevent diffusion and consolidation; PPP has been applied to many sectors across the world with mixed results that, at times, have generated reluctance among policymakers and public managers.

The inherent contract complexity, the level of uncertainty atypical of long-term transactions, and the oligopolistic features of the market are some of the issues making VfM difficult to achieve, especially when risk allocation is influenced by the need to attract private capital. Some relevant contracts across the globe experienced several implementation criticalities due to the need to renegotiate the contract, the failure of the SPV, or excess costs for users or the CA (the affordability issue of PPP). This does not mean that PPP is wrong. Instead, PPP has been used in an incorrect way or by weak institutions. Policies, the institutional context, and contract completeness are salient determinants for the performance of a PPP contract. It is the belief that we need to shift the focus from the "if PPP" perspective to the "how PPP."

Even if PPP is a highly contested policy and countries such as the UK have decided to look for other approaches to deliver infrastructure, it seems that specific alternatives are still vague, especially for infrastructure funded by taxpayers, such as in healthcare and education.

A PPP contract is not only a different procurement route, which bundles together the design, finance, building, maintenance, and delivery of some services. A PPP is a contract to be used to achieve certain policy goals (better and less polluting infrastructure, in certain times and costs, to deliver better and more inclusive services, aligned to the real needs of the society). This is a "go big!"

Bundling together single traditional contracts, with the same level of penalties used in traditional contracts, can't allow the achievement of this "go big." "Horses for courses" should be the approach to follow. To do this it is advisable not only to change the way in which infrastructure is designed and built (for example by using circular economic principles) but also and mainly to conceive the related services in a different way, in order to really tackle societal needs. In this respect, it can be useful to incorporate into the contract performance indicators that can stimulate the EO/SPV to achieve not only output but mainly societal results or outcomes.

In conclusion, to allow and sustain a renewed approach to PPP, based on more balanced and sustainable contracts, where achieving public value becomes the main goal, it is fundamental that both public and private actors evolve. On one hand, public procurement should play a more strategic role with public authorities acting as sophisticated buyers. On the other hand, PPP should be chosen by EOs as a means to pursue their sustainability/ purpose-driven corporate strategies; therefore, they should be keener to include in PPP contracts elements that can really improve contract sustainability and the capacity to generate added value for society.

To get the most from PPP and to use it strategically to achieve greater policy goals, such as the SDGs, it is fundamental to empower and align three dimensions (Figure 6.2).

1. At the macro level, to define clear goals through an explicit policy, which should clearly set the framework and, in particular, the strategic goals beyond the use of PPP, such as the achievement of more VfP and not just macro-economic goals.
2. At the meso level, it is fundamental to ensure a solid environment, made of clear and stable rules to attract investors and reduce perceived risk. Furthermore, the role played by PPP units and development banks is crucial. The role should expand from supporting the policymaker in the design and continuous improvement of the policy and laws, to the preparation of a pipeline of projects, which must be, at the same time:
    a. feasible to attract investors.
    b. VfM, VfP, and affordable from the public perspective.

    Especially in weak institutional contexts, an indirect support of PPP units, through the provision of standard documents, may not be enough and their role should be extended towards a hands-on technical assistance role in the design and implementation of the most complex and strategic contracts. This should also generate a spillover of competences. They should also play an active role in capacity building, to ensure that all the public and private stakeholders are aligned to the policy goals and their achievements. At this level, also the design of adequate BF mechanisms (see Chapter 4), in collaboration with development banks, can be useful to ensure the attraction of needed capital.
3. At the micro level, it is fundamental that contracts are well designed and enforced to achieve policy goals. Again, it must be underlined that standard contracts are important, but it is even more important to create the right competences across the public and private sectors in order to find the right solution for each specific case. For this reason, it is fundamental to find the correct balance between flexibility, needed because each project

is different, and standardization, to allow a more consistent use of PPP and private capital attraction.

A renewed approach to PPP is possible, but only if there is good interaction between all the stakeholders, such as policymakers, public managers, economic players, and investors, think tanks, development banks, consultancies, and law firms. Also, the role of academia (and above all management schools) is fundamental in order to align the competences of such actors to achieve bold goals.

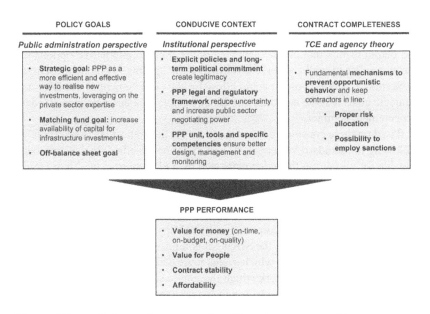

Figure 6.2   Drivers of contractual public-private partnership performance

8.   FROM VALUE FOR MONEY TO VALUE FOR PEOPLE

When approaching PPP, one of the most used and abused expressions is VfM.
    When availability-based PPP contracts were introduced in the UK, within the New Public Management agenda, the main objective for authorities was to achieve affordability and VfM. To support the decision to prefer a PPP

solution rather than a standard procurement contract, a specific analysis was introduced, under the term of VfM analysis, based on the comparison between the costs faced by a procuring authority associated with these two contractual options. In reality, a VfM analysis calculates the present value of the total whole-of-life costs incurred by government for the two alternatives, by also calculating the risks retained under a standard solution. Differently from economic evaluation frameworks, which inherently incorporate public value dimensions, the VfM analysis focuses on operational efficiency and effectiveness, rather than on social welfare.

In other words, in its traditional form, it does not consider the impact on society generated by a procurement/contractual solution. Indeed, if infrastructure is delivered on time, it is not only a matter of cost savings for the authority, but also about delivery of the social benefits associated with the project. Furthermore, in its traditional form, the VfM analysis assumes that the output/results that can be achieved under the two alternative options are the same. When well conceived, following the "go big" approach discussed in Section 7, a PPP contract could allow for the achievement of complex and strategic goals that the authority would not be able to achieve under a standard procurement contract.

Based on these considerations, it is salient for the authorities to be critical in following the standard VfM analysis and to define a methodological approach suitable for measuring the value generated by a PPP contract vis-à-vis a traditional one.

Therefore, to embrace an innovative approach to PPP, more consistent with the current opportunities (such as the refocus of the market towards ESG and II, and the emerging corporate sustainability strategies) and challenges (namely the achievement of the SDGs), it is fundamental to move from a VfM approach to a VfP analysis, which seems more consistent also with the collaborative governance framework which the public sector should move towards. This does not imply only a change in the assessment of the benefits of PPP vis-à-vis a traditional contract but mainly a change in the use of PPP, also thanks to the capacity to play as a sophisticated buyer. Actually moving from a VfM analysis to a VfP analysis should also support and stimulate authorities to approach PPP differently. A VfP framework should consider (as shown in Figure 6.3) different dimensions, such as financial sustainability, environmental impacts, the impact on communities, and the more general impact on socio-economic development.

With reference to the assessment of the value, the shift towards VfP can be done in various forms, but basically by incorporating cost-benefit analysis elements in the standard VfM analysis. For example, to estimate the cost associated to the risk of delay of a standard contract, we have to consider not only the extra cost of keeping a construction site open (as happens in VfM)

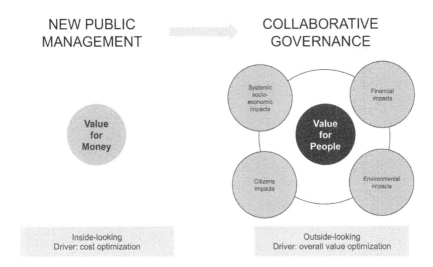

Figure 6.3   The value for people analysis dimensions

but mainly the cost for the users in terms of longer commuting time and/or increased emissions.

Furthermore, if a PPP is used to achieve goals not possible under a traditional contract, because of the lower incentives (such as lack of payment linked to certain social performance indicators) and its unbundled nature, the comparison between a traditional contract and a PPP solution is the wrong approach.

To measure VfP, we need to compare the "as is," generally what the authority can deliver based on a traditional approach, with what society would benefit from a PPP solution, based on enforced contractual clauses to achieve certain social/societal results or outcomes. This is not complex because under this new approach it is not necessary to estimate the risks retained by the authority, which has often generated bias, to support or to discard the PPP option (Vecchi et al., 2021a). This approach, differently from the VfM analysis, which was originally conceived only for availability-based contracts, can and should be used for the assessment of tariff-based PPP, especially if the assessment framework has to act not just as a (frequently ex post) justification of the use of PPP (mainly dictated by macro-economic benefits) but foremost as a trigger to change the approach to PPP. In Figure 6.4 a possible framework for the application of the VfP analysis is shown.

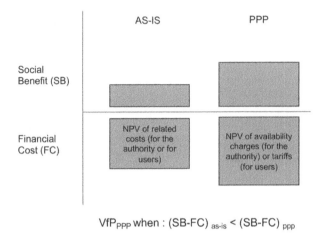

$$\text{VfP}_{PPP} \text{ when : (SB-FC)}_{as\text{-}is} < \text{(SB-FC)}_{ppp}$$

Figure 6.4   The value for people analysis framework

NOTES

1. The content of this chapter is based on Vecchi et al. (2021b).
2. For a detailed analysis of PPP contracts, see Vecchi et al. (2021b).
3. For a deeper understanding of the application of PPP to healthcare, see Vecchi and Hellowell (2018).

References

Abraham, F., & Schmukler, S. L. (2017). Addressing the SME Finance Problem. In *Research and Policy Briefs from the World Bank Malaysia Hub*. https://documents1 .worldbank.org/curated/en/809191507620842321/pdf/Addressing-the-SME-finance -problem.pdf

Agrawal, A., & Hockerts, K. (2021). Impact Investing: Review and Research Agenda. *Journal of Small Business and Entrepreneurship*, *33*(2), 153–181.

Arena, M., Bengo, I., Calderini, M., & Chiodo, V. (2016). Social Impact Bonds: Blockbuster or Flash in a Pan? *International Journal of Public Administration*, *39*(12), 927–939.

Austin, J., Stevenson, H., & Wei-Skillern, J. (2006). Social and Commercial Entrepreneurship: Same, Different, or Both? *Entrepreneurship Theory and Practice*, *30*(1), 1–22.

Austin, J., Gutiérrez, R., Ogliastri, E., & Reficco, E. (2007). Capitalizing on Convergence. *Stanford Social Innovation Review*, *43*, 93–106.

Balandina Jaquier, J. (2016). *Catalyzing Wealth for Change: Guide to Impact Investing*. GIIN, May 2.

Barnett, M. L., Henriques, I., & Husted, B. W. (2020). Beyond Good Intentions: Designing CSR Initiatives for Greater Social Impact. *Journal of Management*, *46*(6), 937–964.

Battilana, J., & Dorado, S. (2010). Building Sustainable Hybrid Organizations: The Case of Commercial Microfinance Organizations. *Academy of Management Journal*, *53*(6), 1419–1440.

Battilana, J., & Lee, M. (2014). Advancing Research on Hybrid Organizing: Insights from the Study of Social Enterprises. *Academy of Management Annals*, *8*(1), 397–441.

Bebchuk, L. A., & Tallarita, R. (forthcoming). Will Corporations Deliver Value to All Stakeholders? *Vanderbilt Law Review*, *75*.

Bilodeau, N., Laurin, C., & Vining, A. (2007). Choice of Organizational Form Makes a Real Difference: The Impact of Corporatization on Government Agencies in Canada. *Journal of Public Administration Research and Theory*, *17*(1), 119–147.

Bloomberg Intelligence. (2021). ESG Assets May Hit $53 Trillion by 2025, a Third of Global AUM. www.bloomberg.com/professional/blog/esg-assets-may-hit-53 -trillion-by-2025-a-third-of-global-aum/

Boardman, A. E., & Vining, A. R. (1989). Ownership and Performance in Competitive Environments: A Comparison of the Performance of Private, Mixed, and State-Owned Enterprises. *Journal of Law and Economics*, *32*(1), 1–33.

Bowen, H. (1953). *Social Responsibility of the Businessman* (Vol. 4). Harper and Row.

Bradshaw, T. K. (2002). The Contribution of Small Business Loan Guarantees to Economic Development. *Economic Development Quarterly*, *16*(4), 360–369.

Brest, P., & Born, K. (2013). When Can Impact Investing Create Real Impact? *Stanford Social Innovation Review*, 22–27.

Bryson, J. M., Crosby, B. C., & Stone, M. M. (2006). The Design and Implementation of Cross-Sector Collaborations: Propositions from the Literature. *Public Administration Review*, *66*(Special Issue), 44–55.

Bugg-Levine, A., & Goldstein, J. (2009). Impact Investing: Harnessing Capital Markets to Solve Problems at Scale. *Community Development Investment Review*, *5*(2), 30–41.

Business Roundtable. (2019). Business Roundtable Redefines the Purpose of a Corporation to Promote "an Economy That Serves All Americans." www .businessroundtable.org/business-roundtable-redefines-the-purpose-of-a -corporation-to-promote-an-economy-that-serves-all-americans

Carbon Disclosure Project. (2019). Major Risk or Rosy Opportunity: Are Companies Ready for Climate Change? CDP. www.cdp.net/en/research/global-reports/global -climate-change-report-2018/climate-report-risks-and-opportunities

Carroll, A. (1979). A Three-Dimensional Conceptual Model of Corporate Social Performance. *Academy of Management Review*, *4*(4), 497–505.

Carroll, A. B. (1991). The Pyramid of Corporate Social Responsibility: Toward the Moral Management of Organizational Stakeholders. *Business Horizons*, *34*(4), 39–48.

Carroll, A. B. (1999). Corporate Social Responsibility: Evolution of a Definitional Construct. *Business and Society*, *38*(3), 268–295.

Carroll, A. B. (2016). Carroll's Pyramid of CSR: Taking Another Look. *International Journal of Corporate Social Responsibility*, *1*(1), 1–8.

Carroll, A. B. (2021). Corporate Social Responsibility: Perspectives on the CSR Construct's Development and Future. *Business and Society*, *60*(6), 1258–1278.

Casalini, F., & Vecchi, V. (2021). From Traditional to Outcome-Based Public-Private Partnerships: Social Impact Bonds. In V. Vecchi, F. Casalini, N. Cusumano, & V. M. Leone (Eds), *Public Private Partnerships: Principles for Sustainable Contracts* (pp. 103–115). Palgrave Macmillan.

Caselli, S., Corbetta, G., Rossolini, M., & Vecchi, V. (2019). Public Credit Guarantee Schemes and SMEs' Profitability: Evidence from Italy. *Journal of Small Business Management*, *57*, 555–578.

Christensen, D. M., Serafeim, G., & Sikochi, A. (2021). Why Is Corporate Virtue in the Eye of The Beholder? The Case of ESG Ratings. *The Accounting Review*. https://doi .org/10.2308/tar-2019-0506

Cohen, R. (2020). Crisis Offers a Chance to Rewrite Accounting to Include Impact. *Financial Times*, July 16. www.ft.com/content/af72b39d-af34-4135-9e4d -f97069075fa4

Convergence. (2020). *The State of Blended Finance*. www.convergence.finance/ reports/sobf2020/assets/The_State_of_Blended_Finance_2020.pdf

Crane, A., Palazzo, G., Spence, L. J., & Matten, D. (2014). Contesting the Value of "Creating Shared Value." *California Management Review*, *56*(2), 130–153.

Cressy, R. (2002). Introduction: Funding Gaps: A Symposium. *The Economic Journal*, *112*(477), F1–F16.

Crosby, B. C., 't Hart, P., & Torfing, J. (2017). Public Value Creation through Collaborative Innovation. *Public Management Review*, *19*(5), 655–669.

Cusumano, N., Casalini, F., & D'Arcangelo, F. M. (2017). EU Financing Policy in the Social Infrastructure Sectors: Implications for the EIB's Sector and Lending Policy – Financed by the European Investment Bank under STARBEI. Veronica Vecchi, Scientific Coordinator.

Da Cruz, N. F., & Marques, R. C. (2012). Mixed Companies and Local Governance: No Man Can Serve Two Masters. *Public Administration*, *90*(3), 737–758.

Dees, J. G. (1998). Enterprising Non Profits. *Harvard Business Review*, *76*(1), 54–67.

Dees, J. G., & Anderson, B. B. (2003). For-Profit Social Ventures. In M. L. Kourilsky & W. B. Walstad (Eds), *Social Entrepreneurship* (pp. 1–26). Senate Hall Academic Publishing.

Della Croce, R., Stewart, F., & Yermo, J. (2011). Promoting Longer-Term Investment by Institutional Investors: Selected Issues and Policies. *OECD Journal: Financial Market Trends*, 1, 145–164. https://read.oecd-ilibrary.org/finance-and-investment/promoting-longer-term-investment-by-institutional-investors_fmt-2011-5kg55b0z1ktb#page1

Dimon, J. (2020). Jamie Dimon: Unless We Change Capitalism, We Might Lose It Forever. *TIME's Davos 2020 Issue*. https://time.com/collection/davos-2020/5764098/jamie-dimon-capitalism/

Directive 2014/23/EU. (2014). Testimony of the European Parliament and the Council.

Doherty, B., Haugh, H., & Lyon, F. (2014). Social Enterprises as Hybrid Organizations: A Review and Research Agenda. *International Journal of Management Reviews*, *16*(4), 417–436.

Drucker, P. F. (1984). Converting Social Problems into Business Opportunities: The New Meaning of Corporate Social Responsibility. *California Management Review*, *26*(2), 53–63.

Eckel, C. C., & Vining, A. R. (1985). Elements of a Theory of Mixed Enterprise. *Scottish Journal of Political Economy*, *32*(1), 82–94.

Elkington, J. (1994). Towards the Sustainable Corporation: Win-Win-Win Business Strategies for Sustainable Development. *California Management Review*, *36*(2), 90–100.

Emerson, J. (2000). *The Nature of Returns: A Social Capital Markets Inquiry into Elements of Investment and the Blended Value Proposition*. Harvard Business School.

Estache, A., Iimi, A., & Ruzzier, C. A. (2009). Procurement in Infrastructure: What Does Theory Tell Us? *World Bank Policy Research Working Paper*, 4994.

EU Commission. (2021). The April 2021 Package on Sustainable Finance. https://ec.europa.eu/info/publications/210421-sustainable-finance-communication_en

Ferrando, A., & Rossolini, M. (2015). SMEs' Access to Credit: Are Government Measures Helpful for Constrained Firms? In S. Caselli, G. Corbetta, & V. Vecchi (Eds), *Public Private Partnerships for Infrastructure and Business Development* (pp. 221–236). Palgrave.

Figueira, I., Domingues, A. R., Caeiro, S., Painho, M., Antunes, P., Santos, R., Videira, N., Walker, R. M., Huisingh, D., & Ramos, T. B. (2018). Sustainability Policies and Practices in Public Sector Organisations: The Case of the Portuguese Central Public Administration. *Journal of Cleaner Production*, *202*, 616–630.

Financial Stability Board. (2018). Evaluation of the Effects of Financial Regulatory Reforms on Infrastructure Finance. www.fsb.org/wp-content/uploads/P180718.pdf

Fink, L. (2020). *Larry Fink's 2020 Letter to CEOs*.

Florida, R. L., & Kenney, M. (1988). Venture Capital, High Technology and Regional Development. *Regional Studies*, *22*(1), 33–48.

Freeman, R. E. (1984). *Strategic Management: A Stakeholder Approach*. Pitman.

Gatti, S. (2013). *Project Finance in Theory and Practice: Designing, Structuring, and Financing Private and Public Projects*. Elsevier.

Gatti, S. (2014). Government and Market-Based Instruments and Incentives to Stimulate Long-Term Investment Finance in Infrastructure. OECD Working Papers on Finance, Insurance and Private Pensions.

Gatti, S., Casalini, F., Colla, P., & Vecchi, V. (2019). An Empirical Analysis of Factors Responsible for the Use of Capital Market Instruments in Infrastructure Project Finance. Working Paper Commissioned by the Asian Development Bank, Asia Infrastructure Insight.

Global Infrastructure Hub. (2020). Fiscal Multiplier Effect of Infrastructure Investment. https://www.gihub.org/infrastructure-monitor/insights/fiscal-multiplier-effect-of -infrastructure-investment/

Grabenwarter, U., & Liechtenstein, H. (2011). In Search of Gamma: An Unconventional Perspective on Impact Investing. *SSRN Electronic Journal.* www.ssrn.com/abstract =2120040.

Grayson, D., & Nelson, J. (2013). *Corporate Responsibility Coalitions: The Past, Present, and Future of Alliances for Sustainable Capitalism.* Stanford University Press.

Hart, O., & Zingales, L. (2017). Companies Should Maximize Shareholder Welfare Not Market Value. *Journal of Law, Finance, and Accounting, 2*(2), 247–275.

Hart, S. L. (2005). *Capitalism at the Crossroads: The Unlimited Business Opportunities in Solving the World's Most Difficult Problems.* Pearson Prentice Hall.

Hellowell, M., Vecchi, V., & Caselli, S. (2014). Return of the State? An Appraisal of Policies to Enhance Access to Credit for Infrastructure-based PPPs. *Public Money and Management, 35*(1).

Hodge, G. A., & Greve, C. (2017). On Public–Private Partnership Performance: A Contemporary Review. *Public Works Management and Policy, 22*(1), 55–78.

Hood, N. (2000). Public Venture Capital and Economic Development: The Scottish Experience. *Venture Capital, 2*(4), 313–341.

Howard, A. (2016). *Painting by Numbers: The Difficulties of Measuring Sustainability.* Market Insights, Schroders, London. www.schroders.com/en/nordics/professional -investor/nordic-insights/expert-magazine/painting-by-numbers---the-difficulties-of -measuring-sustainability/

Jørgensen, T. B., & Bozeman, B. (2007). Public Values: An Inventory. *Administration and Society, 39*(3), 354–381.

Kania, J., & Kramer, M. (2011). Collective Impact. *Stanford Social Innovation Review,* 36. https://ssir.org/articles/entry/collective_impact

Kanter, R. M. (1999). From Spare Change to Real Change: The Social Sector as Beta Site for Business Innovation. *Harvard Business Review.* https://hbr.org/1999/ 05/from-spare-change-to-real-change-the-social-sector-as-beta-site-for-business -innovation

Khan, M., Serafeim, G., & Yoon, A. (2016). Corporate Sustainability: First Evidence on Materiality. *Accounting Review, 91*(6), 1697–1724.

Koppenjan, J. F. M., & Enserink, B. (2009). Public-Private Partnerships in Urban Infrastructures: Reconciling Private Sector Participation and Sustainability. *Public Administration Review, 69*(2), 284–296.

Kortum, S., & Lerner, J. (2000). Assessing the Contribution of Venture Capital. *RAND Journal of Economics, 31*(4), 674–692.

KPMG. (2020). The Time Has Come: The KPMG Survey of Sustainability Reporting 2020. https://assets.kpmg/content/dam/kpmg/xx/pdf/2020/11/the-time-has-come.pdf

Laffont, J.-J., & Tirole, J. (1991). Privatization and Incentives. *Journal of Law, Economics, and Organization, 7*(Special Issue), 84–105.

Lelarge, C., Sraer, D., & Thesmar, D. (2010). Entrepreneurship and Credit Constraints. In J. Lerner & A. Schoar (Eds), *International Differences in Entrepreneurship*. University of Chicago Press.

Lerner, Josh, & Watson, B. (2008). The Public Venture Capital Challenge: The Australian Case. *Venture Capital*, *10*(1), 1–20.

MacNeil, I. (1974). The Many Futures of Contracts. *Southern California Law Review*, *47*(2), 691–816.

Marques, R. C., & Berg, S. (2010). Revisiting the Strengths and Limitations of Regulatory Contracts in Infrastructure Industries. *Journal of Infrastructure Systems*, *16*(4), 334–342.

Marra, A. (2007). Internal Regulation by Mixed Enterprises: The Case of the Italian Water Sector. *Annals of Public and Cooperative Economics*, *78*(2), 245–275.

Mason, C. M. (2009). Public Policy Support for the Informal Venture Capital Market in Europe: A Critical Review. *International Small Business Journal*, *27*(5), 536–556.

Mazzucato, M. (2021). *Mission Economy: A Moonshot Guide to Changing Capitalism*. Penguin.

Meynhardt, T. (2009). Public Value Inside: What Is Public Value Creation? *International Journal of Public Administration*, *32*(3–4), 192–219.

Mooij, S. (2017). The ESG Rating and Ranking Industry; Vice or Virtue in the Adoption of Responsible Investment? *Journal of Environmental Investing*, *8*(1), 331–367.

Moore, M. H. (1995). *Creating Public Value: Strategic Management in Government*. Harvard University Press.

Munro, V. (2020). *CSR for Purpose, Shared Value and Deep Transformation: The New Responsibility*. Emerald Group Publishing.

OECD. (2017). Technical Note on Estimates of Infrastructure Investment Needs. Background Note to the Report Investing in Climate, Investing in Growth. www.oecd .org/env/cc/g20-climate/Technical-note-estimates-of-infrastructure-investment -needs.pdf

OECD. (2018). OECD DAC Blended Finance Principles for Unlocking Commercial Finance for the Sustainable Development Goals. www.oecd.org/dac/financing -sustainable-development/development-finance-topics/OECD-Blended-Finance -Principles.pdf

OECD. (2021a). Government at a Glance 2021. https://doi.org/https://doi.org/https:// doi.org/10.1787/1c258f55-en

OECD. (2021b). Pension Markets in Focus 2021. www.oecd.org/finance/pensionmark etsinfocus.htm

Osborne, S. P., Radnor, Z., Vidal, I., & Kinder, T. (2014). A Sustainable Business Model for Public Service Organizations? *Public Management Review*, *16*(2), 165–172.

Peredo, A. M., & McLean, M. (2006). Social Entrepreneurship: A Critical Review of the Concept. *Journal of World Business*, *41*(1), 56–65.

Popov, A. A., & Roosenboom, P. (2009). Does Private Equity Investment Spur Innovation? Evidence from Europe. Working Paper Series n.1063. European Central Bank.

Porter, M., & Kramer, M. (2006). Strategy and Society: The Link between Competitive Advantage and Corporate Social Responsibility. *Harvard Business Review*, *84*(12), 78–92.

Porter, M., & Kramer, M. (2011). Creating Shared Value: How to Reinvent Capitalism and Unleash a Wave of Innovation and Growth. *Harvard Business Review*, 62–77.

Porter, M., & Kramer, M. (2014). A Response to Andrew Crane et al.'s Article by Michael E. Porter and Mark R. Kramer. *California Management Review, 56*(2), 169–151.

Porter, M., Serafeim, G., & Kramer, M. (2019). Where ESG Fails. *Institutional Investor*, October 16. www.institutionalinvestor.com/article/b1hm5ghqtxj9s7/ Where-ESG-Fails

Rangan, S., Samii, R., & Van Wassenhove, L. N. (2006). Constructive Partnerships: When Alliances between Private Firms and Public Actors Can Enable Creative Strategies. *Academy of Management Review, 31*(3), 738–751.

Reeves, E. (2008). The Practice of Contracting in Public Private Partnerships: Transaction Costs and Relational Contracting in the Irish Schools Sector. *Public Administration, 86*(4), 969–986.

Riding, A., Madill, J., & Haines, G. (2007). Incrementality of SME Loan Guarantees. *Small Business Economics, 29*(1–2), 47–61.

Rodin, J., & Brandenburg, M. (2014). *The Power of Impact Investing: Putting Markets to Work for Profit and Global Good*. Wharton Digital Press.

Santos, F. (2012). A Positive Theory of Social Entrepreneurship. *Journal of Business Ethics, 111*(3), 335–351.

Santos, F., Pache, A. C., & Birkholz, C. (2015). Making Hybrids Work: Aligning Business Models and Organizational Design for Social Enterprises. *California Management Review, 57*(3), 36–58.

Scalet, S., & Kelly, T. F. (2010). CSR Rating Agencies: What Is Their Global Impact? *Journal of Business Ethics, 94*(1), 69–88.

Schoenmaker, D., & Schramade, W. (2019). Investing for Long-term Value Creation. *Journal of Sustainable Finance and Investment, 9*(4), 356–377.

Serafeim, G., & Trinh, K. (2020). A Framework for Product Impact-Weighted Accounts. Working Paper (20-076). www.hbs.edu/impact-weighted-accounts/ Documents/Preliminary-Framework-for-Product-Impact-Weighted-Accounts.pdf

Serafeim, G., Zochowski, T. R., & Downing, J. (2019). Impact-Weighted Financial Accounts: The Missing Piece for an Impact Economy. www.hbs.edu/impact -weighted-accounts/Documents/Impact-Weighted-Accounts-Report-2019.pdf

Sindreu, J., & Kent, S. (2018). Why It's So Hard to Be an "Ethical" Investor. *Wall Street Journal*, September 1. www.wsj.com/articles/why-its-so-hard-to-be-an -ethical-investor-1535799601

Stiglitz, J. E., & Weiss, A. (1981). Credit Rationing in Markets with Imperfect Information. *American Economic Review, 71*(3), 393–410.

Thompson, J. L. (2002). The World of the Social Entrepreneur. *International Journal of Public Sector Management, 15*(4–5), 412–431.

Tirole, J. (2017). *Economics for the Common Good*. Princeton University Press.

UN Deputy Secretary-General Amina Mohammed. (2019). Citing $2.5 Trillion Annual Financing Gap during SDG Business Forum Event, Deputy Secretary-General Says Poverty Falling Too Slowly. Press Release. www.un.org/press/en/2019/dsgsm1340 .doc.htm

United Nations Development Fund for Women. (2015). Empowerment of Women through Microfinance.

van Raak, J., & Raaphorst, A. (2020). From Performance Measurement to Performance Management in the Impact Investment Industry. *Maandblad Voor Accountancy En Bedrijfseconomie, 94*(5/6), 205–217.

Vandekerckhove, W., Leys, J., Alm, K., Scholtens, B., Signori, S., & Schäfer, H. (2012). *Responsible Investment in Times of Turmoil* (Vol. 31). Springer Science and Business Media.

Vecchi, V., & Casalini, F. (2019). Is a Social Empowerment of PPP for Infrastructure Delivery Possible? Lessons from Social Impact Bonds. *Annals of Public and Cooperative Economics, 90*(2), 353–369.

Vecchi, V., & Hellowell, M. (2018). *Public-Private Partnerships in Health: Improving Infrastructure and Technology.* Palgrave Macmillan.

Vecchi, V., Casalini, F., & Gatti, S. (2015). Attracting Private Investors: The EU Project Bond Initiative and the Case of A11 Motorway BT. In S. Caselli, G. Corbetta, & V. Vecchi (Eds), *Public Private Partnerships for Infrastructure and Business Development: Principles, Practices, and Perspectives* (pp. 101–118). Palgrave Macmillan.

Vecchi, V., Hellowell, M., Della Croce, R., & Gatti, S. (2017a). Government Policies to Enhance Access to Credit for Infrastructure-based PPPs: An Approach to Classification and Appraisal. *Public Money and Management, 37*(2), 133–140.

Vecchi, V., Casalini, F., & Caselli, S. (2017b). Impact Investing as a Societal Refocus of Venture Capital: The Perspective of Mature Economies. In V. Vecchi, L. Balbo, M. Brusoni, & S. Caselli (Eds), *Principles and Practice of Impact Investing: A Catalytic Revolution* (pp. 74–92). Routledge.

Vecchi, V., Hellowell, M., & Casalini, F. (2017c). Issues and Trends in Project Finance for Public Infrastructure BT. In S. Caselli & S. Gatti (Eds), *Structured Finance: Techniques, Products and Market* (pp. 127–152). Springer International Publishing.

Vecchi, V., Casalini, F., Cusumano, N., & Leone, V. M. (2020). PPP in Health Care: Trending toward a Light Model: Evidence from Italy. *Public Works Management and Policy, 25*(3), 244–258.

Vecchi, V., Casalini, F., Cusumano, N., & Leone, V. M. (2021a). *Public Private Partnerships: Principles for Sustainable Contracts.* Palgrave Macmillan.

Vecchi, V., Casalini, F., Cusumano, N., & Leone, V. M. (2021b). Value for Money Analysis: Standard and Value-Based Methodologies. In *Public Private Partnerships: Principles for Sustainable Contracts* (pp. 145–164). Palgrave Macmillan.

Visser, W. (2011). *The Age of Responsibility: CSR 2.0 and the New DNA of Business.* John Wiley & Sons.

World Bank. (2015). From Billions to Trillions: Transforming Development Finance. https://thedocs.worldbank.org/en/doc/622841485963735448-0270022017/original/DC20150002EFinancingforDevelopment.pdf

World Bank. (2017). Maximizing Finance for Development: Leveraging the Private Sector for Growth and Sustainable Development. www.devcommittee.org/sites/dc/files/download/Documentation/DC2017-0009_Maximizing_8-19.pdf

World Economic Forum. (2011). The Future of Long-term Investing. www3.weforum.org/docs/WEF_Future_of_Long_term_Investing.pdf

World Economic Forum. (2015). *Blended Finance, Vol. 1: A Primer for Development Finance and Philanthropic Funders.* www3.weforum.org/docs/WEF_Blended_Finance_A_Primer_Development_Finance_Philanthropic_Funders.pdf

World Economic Forum. (2020). Measuring Stakeholder Capitalism: Towards Common Metrics and Consistent Reporting of Sustainable Value Creation.

Zappa, G. (1957). *Le produzioni nell'economia delle imprese* (Vol. 1, p. 37). Giuffrè.

Index

Printed and bound by CPI Group (UK) Ltd, Croydon, CR0 4YY

16/04/2025

14658434-0002